191993

THE
WILLIAM W. COOK FOUNDATION
LECTURES

Earlier volumes in this series were:

FREEDOM AND RESPONSIBILITY IN
THE AMERICAN WAY OF LIFE

by Carl L. Becker

TOTAL WAR
AND THE CONSTITUTION

by Edward S. Corwin

ALTERNATIVE TO SERFDOM

by John Maurice Clark

MEN AND MEASURES
IN THE LAW

by Arthur T. Vanderbilt

THESE ARE *Borzoi Books*
PUBLISHED BY *Alfred A. Knopf* IN NEW YORK

Characteristically American

THE WILLIAM W. COOK FOUNDATION *was established at the University of Michigan to endow a distinguished Lectureship on American Institutions. The donor, William Wilson Cook, long a member of the New York bar, received the degree of Bachelor of Arts from the College of Literature, Science, and the Arts of the University in 1880, and the degree of Bachelor of Laws from the Law School in 1882.*

The lectures presented in this volume are the fifth in the series of lectures under the Foundation. They were delivered in the Rackham lecture halls at the University in November and December 1948, and are published, under a special arrangement between the University and the publisher, as the fifth volume in the lectureship series.

The first volume was Freedom and Responsibility in the American Way of Life, *by Carl L. Becker; the second volume was* Total War and the Constitution, *by Edward S. Corwin; the third was* Alternative to Serfdom, *by John Maurice Clark; the fourth was* Men and Measures in the Law, *by Arthur T. Vanderbilt.*

Characteristically

AMERICAN

Five lectures delivered on the William W. Cook Foundation
at the University of Michigan, November–December 1948

By RALPH BARTON PERRY

Professor of Philosophy, Emeritus
Harvard University

New York   *ALFRED A. KNOPF*   1949

THIS IS A BORZOI BOOK,
PUBLISHED BY ALFRED A. KNOPF, INC.

FIRST EDITION

To my sons,

RALPH BARTON PERRY, Jʀ.,
and
BERNARD BERENSON PERRY

Preface

ANY ATTEMPT to characterize America in a few pages must suffer from many limitations, of which I hope that I am not unaware. The picture is foreshortened, distorted, and lacking in details. It is only one of many portraits which could be painted of the same subject. Whatever is taken to be its character, there will always remain some parts of America that are out of character. It no doubt reflects the bias of the author. Perhaps I should call it "my America." Nevertheless, I have not knowingly set down anything that I have not found; and there is, I believe, some merit in tracing unities and similarities, however incomplete they may be and however selective.

I am grateful to the William W. Cook Foundation for the opportunity to give and to publish these lectures, to my audiences at Ann Arbor for their attention and cordial response, and to my friends at the University of Michigan for the kindness and warmth of their hospitality.

Having been for many years associated with Harvard University, I have accumulated an indebtedness to its resources and to my colleagues — an indebtedness which I cannot measure or repay, but which I can at least acknowledge. In the preparation of the manuscript my secretaries, Catherine F. Malone and Rosamond Hart Chapman, have given me invaluable help and encouragement which I shall not forget.

RALPH BARTON PERRY

Cambridge, Massachusetts
May 2, 1949

Contents

Contents

Characteristically American

I

The American Cast of Mind

1

THERE IS no more teasing and baffling task than the definition of national characteristics. Just as we love to talk over our friends, whether in a kindly or in a malicious spirit, and put their indescribable peculiarities into words, so we turn again and again to such complex and unanswerable questions as, "What is the distinctive genius of the Englishman?" "What is particularly French about Frenchmen?" "What are those German traits which have brought disaster to Europe?" "What is that dark Russian soul on which the future of mankind so largely depends?" These are delightful subjects for discussion because almost anybody can have an opinion without impertinence. There are no experts who have the answers.

What of ourselves? What is it to be American — in thought and deed and feeling? The fascination of such questions lies not only in the uncertainty of the answer, but in its paradoxes. Each nation appears to be a compound not only of many characteristics, but of opposite characteristics. Start with any formula and you will shortly be reminded not only that it is incomplete, but that it is contradicted by what it omits. The Englishman "muddles," but he "muddles *through*"; that is, he gets results. The Frenchman is logical, but he is obsessed with *"l'amour."* The German appears to be a mysterious blend of romanticism and technology, of kindliness and cruelty. The Russian is both autocratic and socialistic. And, similarly,

3

America is, in the same curious fashion, both harshly competitive and humanely idealistic. What is needed, then, is some idea or set of ideas that will not only cover the complex manifestations of American life, but resolve its paradoxes.

A mere enumeration of characteristics does not suffice. Thus Henry Pratt Fairchild, pleading for restricted immigration, in order to preserve that "spiritual reality," that "complex of cultural and moral values" which constitutes Americanism, has listed certain traits on which there would be general agreement: "such things as business honesty, respect for womanhood, inventiveness, political independence, physical cleanliness, good sportsmanship, and others less creditable, such as worship of success, material-mindedness, boastfulness." [1] But how do these and other characteristics *go together*? What is the underlying idea which expresses itself in this aggregate of items and in their paradoxical balance of opposites?

It might be supposed that the continental vastness of America, and its unparalleled variety of climate, natural resources, race and creed, would make such an inquiry both impossible and unprofitable. But the fact is that identity is more easily traced when it dwells amidst variety. It is because there is something common to life in New England and California, Montana and Florida, in the arid deserts of Arizona and the lush Mississippi and Ohio lowlands, in great cities and small towns, that it is possible to find a meaning for Americanism. It is because this thing which is common within our boundaries stops so abruptly at the Mexican border, and so unmistakably though less abruptly at the Canadian border, and begins when one disembarks either at New York or at San Francisco, that it can be detected and set apart from the rest of human life, however similar this life outside may be, taken item

[1] *The Melting-Pot Mistake,* 1926, pp. 201–2.

4

by item. It is because Americans are English, Scotch, Irish, German, French, Spanish, Jewish, Italian, East-European, Asiatic and African that their common Americanism is something else again, something discernible and recognizable, however indescribable. The melting pot has not merely melted: it has cooked a broth with an unmistakable flavor of its own.

In conveying this pervasive and identical character of the American mind it is impossible to make any statement to which exception may not be taken. There is no indivisible Platonic essence of which America is the unique embodiment. There is no American characteristic which is not exemplified elsewhere, or which some Americans do not lack. All that one can possibly claim is that there is among the people of this half-continent taken as a whole, a characteristic blend of characteristics. The cast of the American mind is not a simple quality — but a physiognomy, a syndrome, a form of complexity, a contour, a total effect of the distribution and comparative densities of elements. Nor should one be expected to say on this subject anything that has not been known before. Any claim of original discovery should be distrusted. For America has not hidden its face; its character is not mysterious, but palpable — there are those who would say, flagrant.

Of what elements does a national character, mind, or soul, consist? Not of ideas in the strict sense of the term. The acceptance of attested facts, or of some portion of the body of scientific truth, does not go to the heart of the matter. No doubt most Americans believe that $2 + 2 = 4$, and that the Pacific Ocean is larger than the Atlantic, and that matter is composed of atoms. But Americanism consists not of what Americans believe to be true, but rather of what they believe *in* — their attitudes, their sentiments, their hopes and resolves, their scruples and maxims, or what are sometimes called their "valuations." It is here

5

that Gunnar Myrdal, for example, looks for "the cultural unity" of America — "the floor space upon which the democratic process goes on." He finds such a common ground and sanction in "the fact that *most Americans have most valuations in common* though they are arranged differently in the sphere of valuations of different individuals and groups and bear different intensity coefficients." [2]

2

How America came to be American is a story that has been often told, and a story that can properly be told only by the historian. The present study is an interpretation of America, and not a history. Nevertheless, it is well that it should include a brief summary of the major influences which have formed the American mind and given it its peculiar cast or bias.

In the first place, America developed from a group of colonies. It began as the child of Europe, and while it has achieved maturity and independence it has never lost its parentage and ancestry. Its culture was transplanted after having flowered on other soil. Its thought, therefore, is rarely indigenous, and has always retained something of provincialism even in the manner and tone of its self-sufficiency. It diverged from the main stream of European culture in comparatively modern times, and in the realm of fundamental ideas it still imports more than it exports, thus reversing the balance of trade in the realm of commerce.

Therefore great importance attaches, in the second place, to the ideas which the colonists brought with them,

[2] *An American Dilemma,* 1944, Vol. I, p. xliv. Myrdal's own idea of Americanism is not essentially different from that which is proposed here, though he uses a variety of different expressions such as "practical idealism," "bright fatalism," "rationalism" (in the sense of organized efficiency), "humanistic liberalism," "moral optimism." *Op. cit.,* Introduction.

or which were imported during the early formative period of the nation's history. These consisted of mediaeval European thought; of the literature and science of the Renaissance, and especially of Elizabethan England; and of the "new philosophy" of the Seventeenth and early Eighteenth Centuries, comprising Newton, Locke, Hutcheson, Berkeley, Adam Smith, Descartes, Malebranche, and the broad currents of thought, and especially of political thought, known as the Enlightenment.

In the third place, the colonial mind of America was moulded by Protestant Christianity and in the main by Puritan and Evangelical Protestantism. Except for Maryland, the Catholicism of colonial days was peripheral; and the Catholicism of the later migrations not only came after the main characteristics of the American mind were already crystallized, but did not as a rule reach the upper economic, political and cultural levels of American society.

Fourthly, since the colonies which combined to form the United States were British colonies the institutions of the new nation were fundamentally British. The American Revolution was not a social revolution, or even a political revolution, but a war of liberation, in which the new entity retained the structural characteristics of the parent organism. The very principles invoked to justify the overthrow of British authority were themselves British — Magna Carta and the "higher law," the Common Law, representative parliamentary government, the rights of the individual, the pursuit of happiness. While these original social and institutional forms, together with their associated habits and sentiments, were modified in the course of time, they were never repudiated, but became the heroic memory and sacred legend, the ceremonial symbols, the norm of self-criticism, the core of conservatism, the dream of the future.

Fifthly, the original settlers of America, and many later

7

immigrants, were products of the advancing capitalistic economy. They were yeomen, tradesmen, artisans, professional men, or small landowners, already emancipated from a feudal past — "rising men," jealous of authority, and seeking an opportunity under more favorable conditions to prove the capacity which they felt within themselves. Such men were neither hopeless nor self-satisfied, but ambitious to improve their condition and build for themselves a new society corresponding to their ideas and hopes.

Finally, the philosophical, religious, cultural, and social ideas brought or imported from Europe were modified by the experience of settlement. A sparsely inhabited area of wide expanse, rich in natural resources, presenting formidable but not insuperable obstacles, both stimulated and rewarded effort, and generated a sense of man's power to master nature. The temperate but variable climate, the freedom from economic. pressure and congestion, the rugged and primitive life of the frontier, and the mixture of ethnic types produced men of physical robustness and energy who felt a contempt for the effeminacy and softening luxury imputed to older civilization.

Through the operation of these and other influences the American mind came to possess a specific character which, despite an immense variety of local, ethnic, and economic differences, pervades the whole from coast to coast and from border to border, is recognizable to visitors from abroad, and is sufficiently strong to stamp its imprint on successive generations and waves of immigration.

3

If one were limited to a single word with which to characterize America, one would choose the word "individualism" — used, however, with reservations. If individualism is taken to mean the cult of solitude, or the prizing of those personal traits which set one man apart from his fellows, or are the effect of retreat from the world, then no word could be less appropriate. American individuality is the very opposite of singularity. The people of the United States are highly gregarious and sociable. The individual who holds himself apart, who will not "join," who does not "belong," who will not "get together" and "play the game," who does not "row his weight in the boat," is viewed with suspicion. Americans find silence hard to endure, and if they develop an oddity they make a fad of it so that they may dwell among similar oddities. Their individualism is a *collective* individualism — not the isolation of one human being, but the intercourse and coöperation of many.

At the same time, there is a tonic quality of American life that imbues men with a feeling of buoyancy and resourcefulness. They believe that they can improve their condition, and make their fortunes; and that if they fail they have only themselves to blame. There is a promise of reward, not too remote, which excites ambition and stimulates effort. It is this prospect of abounding opportunity which constitutes that appeal of America abroad which attracted immigrants in colonial days, and still in 1949 causes multitudes in all parts of the world to look wistfully toward our half-closed doors. However harshly America is criticized, foreigners, including the critics themselves, come to America of their own free will. Seen from afar America is a land of promise; and that vision is never wholly obliterated by closer acquaintance, but remains in the form of gratitude and love of country. It is to be assumed that those who come find confirmation of this hopefulness in the reports received from those who have preceded them, and from their own experiences.

It follows that the people of the United States judge, and expect to be judged, by the standard of success, meaning something made of opportunity. There is the opportunity, in the sense of favorable conditions — the "opening," as it is sometimes called — and there is the seizing of the opportunity, the taking advantage of the opening. Success is thought of as the fruit of a marriage between circumstance and action.

American success must be recognized success — not by the God of Things as They Are, but by one's neighbors. Success must be not only measurable, but observed, recorded, applauded, and envied. Hence the close relation of success and publicity, attested by Mark Twain's famous description of the rival boy who went as an apprentice engineer on a Mississippi steamboat:

> That boy had been notoriously worldly, and I just the reverse; yet he was exalted to this eminence, and I left in obscurity and misery. . . . He would always manage to have a rusty bolt to scrub while his boat tarried at our town, and he would sit . . . and scrub it, where we could all see him and envy him and loathe him. . . . When his boat blew up at last, it diffused a tranquil contentment among us such as we had not known for months. But when he came home the next week, alive, renowned, and appeared in church all battered up and bandaged, a shining hero, stared at and wondered over by everybody, it seemed to us that the partiality of Providence for an undeserving reptile had reached a point where it was open to criticism.[3]

This was a local and juvenile social experience, but modern facilities of communication — moving pictures, illustrated magazines, radio, national newspapers, and political conventions — have only enlarged the scale. Applause must follow hard upon achievement; and the volume of applause tends to become the measure of achievement.

The American belief in success is not based on blind faith, or on trust, or on a mere elasticity of spirit, but on experience. Nature makes things big in America — moun-

[3] *Life on the Mississippi*, 1901, pp. 32-4.

tains, rivers, deserts, plants and animals. It is no secret, least of all from the American people, that the little enterprise launched on the banks of the Delaware in 1776 turned out to be a big success. As these people look back over their history, or out upon the life of their times, they see (easily, with the naked eye) American success achieved and in the making; and their confidence seems to them to be justified. They feel themselves to be on the march; toward precisely what is not always clear, but anyway toward something bigger and better.

In America the moving of mountains is not a symbol of the impossible, but a familiar experience. Major Hutton, the assistant engineer of the Grand Coulee Dam, is reported to have said: "If a hard mountain gets in the way, move it. If it's just a soft mountain, freeze the darn thing, forget it, and keep on going." [4] *Keep on going!*

American pride of achievement is local as well as national. Each state and city and region is out to make records — in population, in volume of business, or in the height of its sky-scrapers. If the press report is to be trusted, patriots of the State of Washington now propose to alter the geologic map in order to outstrip their rivals. To quote a certain Dr. C. A. Mittun of that State:

> Man will re-do Mother Nature's work and give Mount Rainier back its prominence in the world of mountains. . . . These two almost unknown sand dunes in Colorado, and that reverse gopher hole in California . . . are in for a bad time. . . . We're going to realize the dream of every Washington mountaineer who scraped the snow from the record-cairn at the top to pile something, anything — snow, rocks, ice — on the crater's rim so our mountain can regain the dignity it deserves.[5]

Here is movement, confidence, verified confidence, visible success, success on a large scale, efficiency, and, let it

[4] John Gunther, *Inside U.S.A.*, 1947, p. 124.
[5] Quoted by the *N.Y. Times*, Aug. 13, 1948, p. 17.

be confessed, a touch of boastfulness. For there is a belief in America, founded half on fiction and half on fact, that Americans owe their major blessings to themselves, rather than to history or inherited institutions — as though they had started from scratch with their bare hands.

It is largely because of a widespread belief in success that competition, while keen and intense, is, as a rule, not deadly or vindictive. No fight is taken to be the last fight. Defeat may not be accepted gracefully, but it is accepted cheerfully, because he who is defeated expects to fight again, with another opponent or on another field of battle. Sometime, somehow, somewhere, he expects to win.

Whether Americans are successful in their pursuit of happiness is another question; the contrary is often asserted. Nor is it clear that they pursue happiness methodically, or have, save for certain sects, such as Christian Science, developed any positive art of happiness. It would perhaps be more correct to say that they believe in the possibility of removing the causes of *un*happiness — pain, poverty, frustration, sickness, old age, and even death. They do not regard unhappiness as the necessary lot of man, to be accepted as a fatality and sublimated in tragic nobility. Even sin is regarded as curable; if not by divine grace, then by psychoanalysis.

American resourcefulness consists to no small extent in the fertility of its intellectual soil. America has become a universal seed bed and nursery for ideas from all the past and from all the world. The American public has become a sort of public at large — the great world-market for ideas. Its immense and voracious literacy creates the greatest aggregate demand for reading matter, for the visual arts, for music, for thoughts and fancies, for anything communicable, in human history. Now while this does convey, and rightly conveys, a suggestion of shallowness and lack of discrimination, it also gives the Americans the sense that they have everything. If they do not make it they can buy it. This does not offend their pride for they feel that they buy it with that which they *have* made.

American self-reliance is a plural, collective, self-reliance — not *"I* can," but *"we* can." But it is still individualistic — a togetherness of several and not the isolation of one, or the absorption of all into a higher unity. The appropriate term is not "organism" but "organization"; *ad hoc* organization, extemporized to meet emergencies, and multiple organization in which the same individuals join many and surrender themselves to none. Americans do not take naturally to mechanized discipline. They remain an aggregate of spontaneities. Such organization develops and uses temporary leaders — "natural" leaders, and leaders for the business in hand, rather than established authorities.

This confidence in achievement through voluntary association and combined effort breeds among Americans a sense of invincible power, a tendency to centrifugal expansion, and a readiness to assume the rôle of a people chosen to head the march of human progress.

The idea of racial superiority did not begin with the political agitators of the South in the Reconstruction Era, nor has it been limited to the context of Negro slavery. It has been applied with equal arrogance to American Indians, to Mexicans, and to the "Mongolians" of the Orient. It was Thomas Hart Benton, voicing the spirit of the advancing westward frontier, and addressing the United States Senate in 1846, who said:

> For my part, I cannot murmur at what seems to be the effect of divine law. I cannot repine that this Capitol has replaced the wigwam — this Christian people, replaced the savages — white matrons, the red squaws — and that such men as Washington, Franklin, and Jefferson, have taken the place of Powhattan, Opechonecanough, and other red men,

13

howsoever respectable they may have been as savages. Civilization, or extinction, has been the fate of all people who have found themselves in the track of the advancing Whites, and civilization, always the preference of the Whites, has been pressed as an object, while extinction has followed as a consequence of its resistance. The Black and the Red races have often felt their ameliorating influence.[6]

The sense of collective power, demonstrated in the rapidity and extent of westward expansion, has led Americans to confuse bigger and better, and to identify value with velocity, area, altitude, and number. Jefferson was concerned to refute the thesis of Buffon that animal and plant life is smaller on the Western continent than in Europe; and he has been proved right. Even human stature has increased in America. The same cult of magnitude has led to that strain of half-believing, half-joking exaggeration which is a feature of American legend and folk-lore. Stories, like everything else, must be "big stories." The hyperbole of the imagination reflects the sense of vital exuberance. When all things are deemed possible, the line between the actual and the preposterous is hard to draw.

This same collective self-reliance, this urge to do something together, gives to the American mind a peculiar aptitude for industrialization and for the development of the technological arts. The American does not readily become a tool, but he is a born user of tools — especially of tools which are a symbol of organized rather than of singlehanded action. The American's love of achievement, his impulse to make and to build, to make faster, to build bigger, to rebuild, to exceed others in making and building, leads to the multiplication and quick obsolescence of gadgets, and the deflection of thought from the wisdom of ends to the efficiency of means.

Publicity in America is valued above privacy. This is

[6] "Superiority of the White Race," *Speech of Mr. Benton of Missouri on the Oregon Question*, Washington, Blair and Rives, 1846, p. 30.

only one of the phenomena which attest the fact that American individualism is collective and not singular. Regimentation did not begin with the New Deal, and government regulation is one of the least of its causes. Americans are made alike by imitation, and by the overpowering pressures of mass opinion and sentiment. Agencies of publicity create and inculcate clichés; national advertising and mass production create uniformity of manners, clothing, and all the articles of daily life. Competition itself tends to uniformity among competitors, since they are matched against one another in like activities, calling for like talents. In order that a competitor may be exceeded he must be exceeded "at the same game."

This tendency to uniformity has been accentuated by modern developments of mass communication, but it is an old and persistent American trait. It was in 1837 that James Fenimore Cooper recorded the following impression of the difference between the English and the Americans:

> The English are to be distinguished from the Americans by greater independence of personal habits. Not only the institutions, but the physical condition of our own country has a tendency to reduce us all to the same level of usages. The steamboats, the overgrown taverns, the speculative character of the enterprises, and the consequent disposition to do all things in common aid the tendency of the system in bringing about such a result. In England a man dines by himself in a room filled with other hermits, he eats at his leisure, drinks his wine in silence, reads the paper by the hour; and, in all things, encourages his individuality and insists on his particular humours. The American is compelled to submit to a common rule; he eats when others eat, sleeps when others sleep, and he is lucky, indeed, if he can read a paper in a tavern without having a stranger looking over each shoulder.

At the same time Cooper reported the observation that "the American ever seems ready to resign his own opinion to that which is *made to seem* to be the opinion of the public." [7] In other words, the sanction of public opinion is invoked as an authority so coercive upon the individual that its name carries weight even in the absence of the fact.

4

The characteristic American blend of buoyancy, collective self-confidence, measuring of attainment by competitive success, hope of perpetual and limitless improvement, improvising of method and organization to meet exigencies as they arise, can be illustrated from various aspects of American life, some fundamental and some superficial: though which is fundamental and which superficial it would be difficult to say. This same blend of traits will at the same time serve to account for certain American ways which seem to non-Americans paradoxical, if not objectionable.

Thus Americans are at one and the same time lawabiding and lawless. They live within a frame of law, and seem often to make a fetish of their written constitution. The law is the usual road to public office, and the lawyers are perhaps the most influential members of the community, with the businessmen running them a close second. The business lawyer is the higher synthesis of the two. At the same time Americans have a certain contempt for the law, as something which they have made, and which they sometimes take into their own hands. As in the case of the Prohibition Law, one of the accepted methods of changing the law is to break it. Americans employ lawyers to enable them to evade the law, or at any rate to mitigate its inconveniences.

Americans are highly litigious. Opposing lawyers engage

[7] James Fenimore Cooper, *Gleanings in Europe*, 1837, Vol. II, pp. 248–9.

in lively combat; prosecuting attorneys score their convictions and acquire thereby a prestige that may start them on the road to the Presidency; criminal lawyers score their acquittals. Appeal follows appeal from court to court; but while a negative verdict is not lightly accepted, it usually *is* accepted after every legal resort has been exhausted. Americans are more insistent in claiming legal rights than scrupulous in respecting them: in other words, they tend to assume that each will look after his own — which he usually does.

5

American politics are harshly competitive but rarely bloody or fatal. Candidates do not, as in England, "stand" for office — they "run" for office. Major campaigns are conducted as though the survival of the country were at stake; but nobody really means it. On the morrow the defeated candidate "concedes" his defeat and congratulates the victor whom the day before he has slain with invectives. As in sport, the punch is followed by the handshake. A government based on division of powers has become a struggle between powers — between the legislative and executive branches, or between the upper and lower houses of Congress. Even party solidarities tend to dissolve amidst the rivalries of persons, lobbies and pressure groups. And yet there is a saving grace, which somehow triumphs over dissension — a saving grace which is in part an incurable sense of humor, in part a common underlying faith, but in the main the belief that there is enough for everybody, and that what is lost today can be regained tomorrow. Disputes among optimists rarely become irreconcilable conflicts.

The world would be glad to discover the key to the foreign policy of the United States, which it views with mingled hope and distrust. There is no key; but the Amer-

17

ican mentality here described may throw some dim light on a question which is of no little importance for the future of mankind.

The traditional isolationism, which is still to be reckoned with, was originally based on fear of becoming embroiled in the affairs of a Europe whose yoke had been cast off; and this cautious isolationism was confirmed by the fact that later waves of immigration were composed of persons who, having for one reason or another turned their backs on Europe, desired to keep them turned. But these motives of distrust have gradually been superseded by a sense of self-sufficiency. While the surpluses of production have led to a growing recognition of the need of world markets, the average American businessman is still interested primarily in the domestic market; and while the experience of the present century has brought home the menace of world-war, the fact remains that American territory has not been invaded or seriously threatened with invasion for 130 years, so that those who reside in the interior of a wide continent bounded by two wide oceans still feel secure at home. The airplane and the atomic bomb have modified this attitude; but whereas Europeans know from *experience* that for better or worse they are dependent on the rest of the world, Americans still have to be *persuaded* that this is the case, and they do not always stay persuaded.

Opposed to this sense of continental self-sufficiency and disposition to isolationism there is a missionary spirit which inclines to adventure abroad: a belief, more or less justified, that what is good for the United States is good for everybody, and should be extended to other peoples, whether they like it or not, and whether or not they are ready to receive it. Americans are disposed to "sell" their goods abroad, whether automobiles, typewriters, moving pictures, democracy, or various brands of Christianity.

There is a readiness to embark on far-flung enterprises without a full recognition of their costs; or to talk about them without being prepared to follow through. Bold utterances are discounted at home, but when taken at their face value abroad they have often led to disappointment and resentment, by friends as well as enemies. It is not that Americans do not mean what they say, but that they do not always weigh their words and the implications of their words. Americans speak freely and lightly. Add to this the fact that our foreign policy reflects all the uncertainties arising from differences between Congress and the Executive, and from changing party majorities, and it is small wonder that other nations have learned to keep their fingers crossed.

The foreign policy of the United States must always be close to the electorate, and there is never a time when a nation-wide election is more than two years away. A large section of the press is commercially motivated, and caters to emotion and prejudice in order to compete for circulation. All publicity agencies — radio, cinema, and forum — tend similarly to quantity production and to mass appeal.

That, nevertheless, public policy should on the whole and in the long run have been judged sound by the verdict of history evidently requires explanation; whether it be by a Providence that watches over drunkards and democracies, or by a basic intelligence and good sense which makes the American people as a whole receptive to the enlightenment which spreads from their thoughtful minority by a sort of osmosis. Somehow, in the end, the sober second thought tends to prevail.

Once the people of the United States feel themselves fully committed to an enterprise their virtues come into play, and their very weaknesses become sources of strength. They discover natural leaders, invent techniques, improvise organizations, and are imbued with a confident determination to win. And in so far as they are impregnated with a sense of human solidarity, they can contribute to international organization their peculiar faculty for combining effort with the cheerful acceptance of temporary defeat, and their inexhaustible confidence that what needs to be done *can* be done, even on a world-wide scale, and whatever the odds against it.

6

There are two peculiarly American institutions, American sport and the American college, which will serve further to illustrate the character of the American mind. American sport is essentially competitive whether between teams or between coaches or managers; Americans play to win. In international sports such as tennis, golf, and track athletics, Americans are distinguished by their aggressiveness and by a preparation and training so intensive that the line between the amateur and the professional is hard to draw. American football, peculiarly American in its mixture of physical force with elaborate strategy and the opportunism of the "huddle," largely occupies the attention of the public during the autumn months; following hard upon the close of the baseball season, which culminates in an inter-league contest which Americans modestly designate as the "World Series." Both of these sports are struggles for victory in which the score is the main thing, and in which courage, effort, and the will to win are esteemed above grace, or form, or adherence to a code. One may say that such and such "is or is not cricket"; but in America one does not say, in a similar sense, that anything is or is not baseball or football.

In both sports the "official" is of major importance. It is the business of the player to defeat the opponent, leaving it to the official to impose the rules; so that the game not infrequently resolves itself into a double contest, the contest between the opposing teams and the contest between the players or their partisans and the umpire or referee. Penalties are taken as a matter of course. No one thinks less of a player who breaks the rules owing to his excessive zeal; there is, in fact, an ambiguous zone between the legal and the illegal. Sportsmanship means not scrupulous observance of the rules but acceptance of the penalty, together with team-work and a spirit of camaraderie. Rules and their enforcers are regarded as a disagreeable necessity, but as a necessity nonetheless. The exuberance of the game leads to a constant encroachment on the rules, which must then be reënforced by new rules, requiring a corps of experts for their interpretation, until a full-dress football or baseball game requires four or more such custodians of the law.

American sport is marked not only by this competitive zeal but by the large place which it fills in the public consciousness throughout all classes of society. An army of scribes is required to record for posterity every detail of major contests. Scarcely a game is played in which some record is not broken, and teams which fail to win are offered the consolation of breaking the record of defeat. There are baseball and football players who have achieved immortality because of having committed outstanding "boners" (referring to the comparative absence of gray matter in the skull); for after all, fame is fame. Every newspaper has a staff of sports writers and cartoonists, and their idiom is one of the principle areas of speech in which English is ceasing to be English.

7

Turning from sports to higher education may seem an abrupt transition — but not in America. There are colleges whose names are known to most Americans only as the names of football teams; and which are completely forgotten at the end of the season, except for echoes of past athletic triumphs, and reports of prospects for the season to come. College athletics tend to become "big time"; indeed, their development has reached such proportions that coaches are often more important than professors, and students frequently choose their college for its athletic rather than for its academic prowess. There is, it is true, a group of institutions known as the "Ivy Colleges," which are supposed to be distinguished by their comparative emphasis on scholastic standards and intellectual virtues. But the sports writers who invented the name impart to it an unmistakably derisive tone; the term "ivy" conveying the suggestion of respectable antiquity coupled with self-righteousness and anemia.

"Collegiatism," beginning in secondary schools, imparts a common flavor of Americanism to colleges and universities of every type — Jesuit colleges, sectarian Protestant colleges, urban and rural colleges, state universities, even the older privately endowed Eastern universities originally modeled upon the universities of Britain or Germany.

"Collegiatism" suggests the identification of the college with the spirit of American sport. Earnest effort to win is called the "old college try." College loyalty to athletic teams, incited by bands and cheer-leaders, is a typical manifestation of organized mass-enthusiasm; not for ideas but for "our side," for improvised symbols, for synthetic "traditions." There is a will to "do or die," which can be methodically created, and transposed without serious difficulty from one object to another. The college hero, like the athletic hero, is eminent not for his qualities, but for his "popularity," within the college community itself, and through the assistance of the press and the continuing interest of alumni, in the larger local or even national community.

In their non-athletic activities American colleges manifest something of the same competitive spirit, intensity of effort, and capacity for organization. The steady increase in the numbers of students who complete secondary education and then proceed to college or university cannot be explained by intellectual aspiration merely, or by the necessity of preparing for a professional career. "Going to college" signifies improving one's position in the world — "getting ahead," as it is so fitly expressed. Since students often attend college at a distance from their homes, and since the cost of a college education is reduced to a minimum by scholarships, remission of tuition, and by "earning one's way," this is one of the chief forms of American opportunity, and of that mobility of American life by which differences of locality, race, and economic class are obliterated.

The academic and curricular activities of American colleges reflect some of these same general traits in the immense variety of institutions, the recording of grades, the multiplication of administrative agencies, the chaotic mixture of vocational and liberal studies, the frequent changes in requirements for admission and graduation, the competition for numbers and prestige. Even in the field of research it is possible to trace similar tendencies. The college or university makes it possible to combine learning and the arts with livelihood, so that not only scholars, but even poets, painters and musicians are likely to earn their living by an academic job.

8

American scholarship tends to be marked by earnest ambition and by the multiplication of facilities, and to be measured by the volume rather than by the quality of production; which perhaps accounts for the fact that America is notable for the number of her scientists of the second rank, and for her development of useful applications, rather than for individual genius and epoch-making originality.

America has not consciously disparaged intellectual pursuits. The essential quality of American enterprise, set forth in characteristically flamboyant rhetoric, appears in the following appeal to professional men to settle in Illinois in 1837:

> There are those to whom, in speaking of the advantages of a new country, we can point to higher and nobler inducements than the mere acquisition of worldly goods — many who are engaged in the noble employment of cultivating and improving the human intellect, and desire a broad and ample field upon which to exert the energies of that immortal mind with which Providence has blessed them.
>
> To those we would speak in the language of affectionate regard, and would endeavour to convince them that, if they desire distinction in that branch of science to which their attention has been directed — if eminence in their profession is the object of their wishes, that they have only to summon up moral courage to enter boldly on a scene of action which will inevitably lead to happy and glorious results. But they must be endued with the spirit of lofty determination and noble resolution — a determination that will brave all obstacles — a resolution that will support them under all privations — not that weak and sickly resolution that every difficulty discourages, and every obstacle disheartens; but that bold and manly resolution which, fixing its eagle eye upon the topmost height, determines to reach the destined mark, and, like the thunder-bearer of Jove, when storms and tem-

24

pests beat around, soars higher and loftier, and sustains itself by the force and sublimity of its own elevation.[8]

It would be a mistake, then, to suppose that the American idea of success is limited to material success. That which is characteristically American is not the exclusion of art, literature, science, and religion by the pursuit of wealth, but the introduction *into* art, literature, science, and religion of something of the same spirit and attitude of which the pursuit of wealth affords the most notable or notorious manifestation: not the drowning of culture by the hum of industry, but the idea, to quote a familiar and no doubt apocryphal Chicagoism, of making culture hum. And so — material success, yes, but any kind of success, with no prejudice whatever against cultural attainment provided it can be recognized and measured as success. The standard is not essentially sordid or commercial, but it is essentially competitive, whether that consists in beating records or in beating other competitors.

Culture tends to be thought of in America as a commodity which can be advertised, produced, distributed, and consumed: requiring only earnestness and organization. In 1924, when this strange phenomenon reached its peak, the Chautauqua Movement reached an estimated 35,000,000 people in 12,000 American towns. Being lectured to, the most painless form of learning, and an old American custom, made famous by Emerson, is still in vogue; and has been supplemented rather than superseded by more modern methods of reaching ever bigger, if not better, audiences.

In literature and the fine arts there is the same earnestness of endeavor and eclectic hospitality that appear in the field of learning. Americans are willing, as they say, to "try anything once." Cultural fashions imported from

[8] *Illinois in 1837*, anonymous, edited by H. L. Ellsworth, 1837, p. 142.

abroad have a quick and wide vogue, and tend to obscure what is indigenous. America is the great market for ideas, and if ideas were paid for in dollars there would be no problem of the balance of trade. There is an impatience to obtain results, to secure recognition, to make sales, and a corresponding reluctance to submit to discipline and training in craftsmanship. There is, in the cultural arts, an ominous trend to mass appeal and quantity production parallel to that so notably evident in the industrial arts.

American literature tends to the "book of the month," and the "best seller": that is, to popular uniformity and to success measured by numbers and profit — all the way from "nonfiction," through fiction to magazines, whether slick or pulp, and to the syndicated columns of the press. Architecture tends to monumental public buildings, skyscrapers, or railway stations. In the field of the pictorial arts Americans excel in news photography and the advertising allure of the nylon stocking. Those cultural manifestations of which sophisticated Americans feel most ashamed, and which are most despised and enjoyed abroad — the products of Hollywood, the comic strip, the soap opera — are, however low in the artistic scale, unmistakably American. Perhaps it would not be untrue to say that the meaning of life for the mass of the American people is revealed not in the tragedy, nor in the comedy of manners, but in the melodrama or "western" — with its dash and excitement, its galloping horses or speeding automobiles, its pursuits and hairbreadth escapes, its prodigious feats, its wicked villain and 100% pure heroine — and above all its *happy ending*.

The Americanism which the melodrama illustrates is not, however, merely a bad form of art, but a serious interpretation of life: a recognition of the force of evil and of the inertia and indifference of inanimate nature, coupled with an ideal of the good and a belief in man's power to achieve it by the contrived and combined efforts of individuals. For, after all, why should things not end happily, *if possible,* as most Americans believe to be the case.

It is natural that a country which is so busily engaged in harnessing multiple energies to diverse and incoherent ends should be a noisy country; and that it should respond to ragtime and jazz. "Who can say," asks a critic of Negro music, "that it does not express the blare and jangle and the surge too, of our national spirits?" [9]

9

Other illustrations of American individualism are afforded by religious and philosophical developments, both of which will receive further attention. The conditions of American life are peculiarly favorable to that multiplication of sects which is inherent in Christian Protestantism. Every known religious cult has been transplanted and has flourished on American soil; and indigenous varieties have been added. Even liberalism, non-sectarianism humanism, and atheism have become sects. The American sees no reason why religions should be inherited from the past. Cults of all sorts, religious, non-religious, anti-religious, and near-religious, spring up wherever two or three are gathered together; they are born, wax and wane, and sometimes die. Diverse philosophies have been freely introduced from abroad and acclimated to the peculiar bias of the American mind.

10

American manners have received much unfavorable comment both from visitors to America and from the visited in foreign lands. The American frontiersman trav-

[9] James Weldon Johnson, *The Book of American Negro Poetry,* 1922, p. xv.

eled light and divested himself of formal courtesies, as well
as of other trappings of older civilization. His manners as
well as his housing, his furniture, his dress, his habits of
life, reflected the primitive character of his environment.
The hunter and trapper, the migratory settler, the cattle-
man and miner, possessed little of the graciousness of the
Old World peasant. The stimulus to ambition and the
fluidity of American society have given to American manners something of the character of the parvenu, whose rise
in fortune and power has outstripped his capacity to wear
them becomingly.

American gregariousness and craving for recognition have
conduced to exhibitionism and invasions of privacy. The
harshness of competition has conduced to a willingness to
accept with too great equanimity the defeat of the opponent, who is conceived as having had his chance and failed
in a fair fight. Contacts with the refinements of Europe and
Asia have begotten a sense of inferiority, an over-compen-
sation, and a contempt for that of which one feels the lack.
Hence the typical American, as characterized sympathet-
ically by Mark Twain and superciliously by foreign critics:
harshness of voice, loudness of speech, bombast, provincialism, naïveté, vulgarity, immaturity, insensitiveness — in a
word, crudity.

But there is another side of the picture. Even the frontier
itself has begotten a certain ceremoniousness, an eloquence
and exuberance of rhetoric, a chivalry toward women, a
tendency to carry to the excess of sentimentality certain
gentler feelings, such as the mother-cult, and the protective
attitude to children and animals.

There is a sense in which Americans have the best manners in the world, and it is in this sense that their manners
reflect most profoundly the essential character of Americans. The American is often found distasteful because he is
disposed instantly, or on short acquaintance, to disclose

not only his name, but his business and his biography. He gives himself away — prematurely, it is felt. He does not wait to assure himself that his confidences are desired; nor does he insist on reciprocity. But that which underlies this trait, intrusive as it may sometimes be, is the fact that the American has nothing to conceal, and assumes that this is equally the case with others. There is a basic trust and a desire to establish a friendly atmosphere. This expresses not only a repugnance to silence and aloofness, but a desire to put the other man at his ease. The American impulse is to introduce oneself to everybody and everybody to everybody else, and so to include everybody in the group of social intercourse. At times annoying, yes; sometimes insufferably boring. At times, excessively hearty and familiar. But it is a manifestation of good will and generosity, and as such it is a major condition of that collective self-confidence and capacity for united effort, which is the major virtue of the American character.

11

The last half-century has witnessed an increasing disillusionment and self-criticism, especially in American literature. There is a sophisticated élite which scoffs at such Americanisms as are here described. But one does not find the peculiarities of a nation in its sophistication. Sophistication tends to be the same among all persons and peoples. To find what is characteristic of America one must look for its naïveté; for that unself-critical self which its self-criticism criticizes; for the illusions from which it seeks emancipation.

True satire is true. It must reveal the dark side of the picture; and it must go to the heart of the matter. It must disclose the characteristic faults which spring from the characteristic virtues. The latest of these satires, Evelyn

Waugh's *The Loved One,* is telling because it hits the
target near the bull's eye. It portrays American sentimentality, shallowness, faddism, ostentation; the substitution
of packaged commodities for standards of excellence, and
of packaged opinions for thinking; the displacement of
the individual by the type moulded by the mass influence of
radio, cinema, and press — the American girl "dressed and
scented in obedience to advertisements"; [10] or, as Emerson
had remarked a century ago: "We come to wear one cut of
face and figure, and acquire by degrees the gentlest as-
sinine expression." [11] These are not accidental defects; they
spring from those very conditions and traits which create
the power and constitute the merit of America.

The criticism of American life by American writers, the
literature of disillusionment, beginning in the last quarter
of the Nineteenth Century, has depicted the dark and inhumane side of the frontier — the brutalities of lynch-law,
and the wanton waste of natural resources; the cost of the
struggle for success to those who fail, or barely survive; the
drab existence of those who live in the backwaters and stagnant pools — of those "simple natures that fasten themselves like lichens on the stones of circumstance and
weather their days to a crumbling conclusion"; [12] the
sham, the hollowness, the pettiness of lower middle-class
life in the American small town.

Much of this criticism is simply a frank acknowledgment
that Americans share the ills that flesh is heir to, and is no
more than the American manifestation of the "realistic" or
"naturalistic" impulse common to all the literatures of the
epoch. It is significantly American, however, in that the
tribal mores which it challenges are the American mores.

[10] 1948, p. 134.

[11] "Self-reliance," *Essays, First Series,* Riverside Edition, 1884, p. 56.

[12] Theodore Dreiser, "The Lost Phoebe," *Free, and Other Stories,* 1918,
p. 114.

It selects for attack the peculiar American propensity to romantic optimism: self-confidence carried to the point of complacency and blindness; confusion between the ideal possible, and the real achievement; attention to the hopeful symptoms, and neglect of the more ominous.

It is significantly American that America should have bred its own critics, and that these should have opened the closets and revealed the skeletons. Americans have not hesitated to throw stones despite the fact that they live in a glass house. Their family quarrels are seen and overheard by their neighbors throughout the world. This in itself suggests the American passion for publicity and the open life. No conspiracy of silence, no code of reticence is possible in America; there are no secrets. And at the same time there is a feeling that America has nothing to hide, nothing to fear from disclosure. American self-criticism expresses a sense of sin. It has rarely been cynical or despairing, but has proved the tenacity of American ideals and their exacting demands. Americans both have a conscience and violate it. The brutal treatment of Indians and Orientals, the Mexican War and the exploitation of Mexicans, Negro slavery and all its long painful sequel, were and are clear violations of American principle. Imperialistic expansion was and is inconsistent with the American creed of self-determination. The system of unrestricted free enterprise with its ruthless competition, its corporate monopolies, and its amassing of great fortunes, was and is inconsistent with the humanitarian and equalitarian maxims of democracy. America has not succeeded in preventing its right hand from knowing what its left hand was doing, or failing to do.

12

In this characterization of the mind of America no attempt is made to chart its future, or even to take account of the changed conditions by which it is at present, no doubt, being altered. For over half a century it has been predicted that the American as here described would soon be extinct. There is no longer a Western frontier, opportunity is narrowed, class conflict is sharply accentuated, the population has become in larger proportion urban and industrial, imperialism and internationalism have superseded isolationism, culture has matured and ripened. But even though all this is in some sense true, America does not seem to know that it has lost its identity. The remarkable thing is not that America should change and cease in the old sense to be American, but that despite change it should remain so much the same. Perhaps this is because the original American idea embraced change, so that Americans of the Seventeenth, Eighteenth and Nineteenth Centuries, were they here to see, would recognize the America of today as the fulfilment of their own prophecy.

Americanism is not a static thing, crystallized by habit, custom, authority, and dogma, but a broad and flexible purpose which is adaptable to altered conditions, and which moves to new frontiers when old frontiers have been left behind. The belief, the will, the faith which is American is no worship of the past, no assurance that all is perfect in the eternal constitution of things, or in another world, but a conditional faith: *we can if we try,* and put our minds and our hands to it, and unite our action. It is not an easy optimism — a faith that moves mountains by simply wishing and believing, or by invoking supernatural agencies, but an inventive optimism, which moves mountains by learning how and applying the necessary leverage. It is utopian in its dreams, but does not confuse dreams with the actual state of affairs, and is prepared to earn rewards and not have them handed out.

This faith is justified to Americans by the fact that mountains *have* been moved. This faith, like all faith, exceeds the limits of past experience, but only because past experience itself has proved the immense resources of the implemented human will. It is a faith which does not easily accept impossibilities because so many impossibilities have proved to be possible. It is a faith, therefore, which is peculiarly suited to change: welcoming change both as affording an opportunity of advance, and as requiring new moves with which to meet those of the evil adversary. Americanism is not dismayed by the uncertainty of the future, or by the surprises of the perpetually unfolding present.

II

The Development
of American Thought

1

THE TERM "thought" may be taken to mean a concern with general ideas which philosophy shares with the natural and social sciences, with literature and criticism, with religion, and even with popular belief and common sense. Without this distinction between philosophy proper and philosophy improper, it is impossible to determine the importance of philosophy in America. It is sometimes said that the American mind is comparatively unphilosophical, or that philosophy exercises a comparatively slight influence on American life. This is perhaps true if by philosophy is meant pure, abstract, or speculative philosophy — which has tended in America to be "academic," in the double sense of the professional and the irrelevant. It is doubtful if even William James and John Dewey can be said to be as profoundly American as Descartes and Bergson are French, as Hobbes, Locke, and Mill are English, or as Kant, Hegel, and Nietzsche are German. This is in part due to the fact that American philosophy is European in origin and tradition; but also to the fact that philosophy has for the most part influenced American life indirectly through the medium of religion, morality, education, science, politics, economics, or literary and aesthetic criticism. If by philosophy is meant the appeal to general ideas and basic principles in any branch of culture, then America is perhaps of all nations not the least but the *most* philosophical.

The proof of any doctrine, philosophical or non-philosophical, lies in the objective evidence which can be cited in its support. In proportion as thought is faithful to its essential cognitive purpose it will endeavor to transcend the accidents of its origin, and to emulate the universality so notably achieved in mathematics and the so-called exact sciences. Nevertheless it will inevitably reflect prejudices and prejudgments: it will start with some peculiar mental inheritance; it will give special attention to certain questions rather than to others; it will approach the universal truth from some peculiar starting-point of origin, and therefore follow some peculiar path. Thus there is an inescapable national bias, which is both cause and effect — a self-confirming bias which once having come to pass has grown by its own exercise. It lies below the level of formal expression. It is an attitude, an inarticulate premise, an undefined standard which since it is deeper than art, literature, politics, business, science and philosophy, colors them all alike, and governs the judgments and sentiments of everyday life and of the common man.

It would be an egregious error to suppose that this national bias — this Americanism — is the sole or even the principal source of any single branch of American culture. At best it can only describe what is American about it. A painter, a poet, a scientist, a statesman, a businessman, a professor of philosophy, has his own vocation and his own threads of connection with the past and the present, both at home and abroad; and he also has himself, his own talent and inventiveness — or possibly genius.

Emphasis on the national characteristics of thought must not be allowed to obscure *contemporary* characteristics. It is at least questionable, for example, whether the philosophy of America in the Nineteenth Century does not have more in common with European philosophy in the same century than it has with American philosophy in the Seventeenth Century. The fact is that it is possible to define many similarities — epochal, geographical, linguistic, ethnic. They cannot be reduced to one, such as national, except under the influence of a nationalism which is itself a national bias. A graphic representation of philosophical similarities would be composed of many intersecting circles drawn from different centers, and having different diameters all the way from the personal philosophy of a particular man in some phase of his development to the human philosophy embracing all men of all times and places.

2

In the realm of ideas America has been peculiarly receptive. Whatever barriers have been erected against the importation of physical commodities, or in later years against immigration, the door has been open wide to cultural influences from all quarters. Given the circumstances of the settlement of the country and the varied composition of its population this could not well have been otherwise. Those who have settled here from different parts of the world have brought ideas with them. Contacts have been maintained between settlers or immigrants and their places of origin. A rising level of literacy, constantly improving means of communication, and a lingering provincialism, however much resented, have created in America an extraordinary intellectual hospitality. This has been reconciled with national pride by the idea that nothing is too good for America, that America must have the best — the latest model whether made at home or imported from abroad. At the same time there has emerged from all this variety of impacts a characteristic American response — a selective response, which tries all things but assimilates or rejects; a resultant of many causes, which itself acts as a cause.

The least misleading name for this selective response, this American bias, is "collective individualism." The term "individualism" signifies the irreducible reality, the genuine causal efficacy, and the ultimate worth, of the individual. It must *not* be taken to imply the isolation or exclusiveness of one individual but the co-presence, the togetherness, the association, the interaction, the organization, of many. The term "collective" must be taken to mean the manyness of distinct individuals, and not their fusion, or their control or replacement by any kind of corporate entity or institution such as race, nation, state or historical or social force. The individual in question is that unit of human life, that real person, denoted by the singular form of the personal pronoun and enumerated in the census. Collective individualism is the conscious philosophy, or fundamental belief, or unconscious presupposition, which credits such individuals, whether in competition or in concert, with a power to modify their environment and subject it to their ends; which endorses their claim to be the masters and beneficiaries of social institutions; and which credits them with a hand in the making of history.

This collective individualism gives a characteristic accent to American thought. Amidst the wide ranges of philosophical ideas which Americans have inherited from the past, or received from abroad, or drawn from their own minds, the ideas which have been uttered with most conviction, which have enjoyed the widest vogue, which have taken root and borne fruit, have been ideas which are consistent with this individualism. The characteristic modifications of ideas imported from abroad have been in the direction of this individualism. History thus presents us with a sort of experimental test. The very range of stimuli, whether presented by the past, or by contemporary thought throughout the world, or by the fecundity of the American mind itself, has served to bring out more clearly the consistency of the American response.

3

The principal channel by which Christianity was imported into America was that form of Calvinistic-Protestant belief which is commonly known as Puritanism. The settlement of America, including not only New England but the Middle and Southern colonies, was largely a result of the Puritan Revolution in England and Scotland, and the struggles between Protestantism and Catholicism, and between the Reformed or Calvinistic, and the Lutheran, forms of Protestantism on the continent.

In the course of its development in America Protestantism was gradually divested of those tenets of Calvinism which conflicted with the buoyancy and individual self-reliance of a frontier society. The famous "Five Points" of Calvinism, with their insistence on human helplessness and depravity, became infamous. Puritanism was identified with an inhumane view of divine vindictiveness, with bigotry and intolerance, and with ecclesiastical tyranny; and so construed, it was rejected. In the course of time it came to be regarded as a hereditary mental disease for which a cure was sought in psychoanalysis — an anti-Americanism lying at the heart of America, and the cause of a peculiarly American psychosis.

At the same time there was another Puritanism, which was congenial to American individualism, and was absorbed into the American tradition. This American version of Puritanism comprised the discipline of the will; the emphasis on personal accountability; the attributing of failure to moral weakness rather than to heredity or circumstance; the contractual theory of institutions, by which even God was held to his bargain; the congregational form of church polity; the recognition of the hard facts of evil. Especially congenial to the individualistic temper of American life was the Calvinist sanction of prudence and worldly success, which associated the accumulation of wealth with the virtues of thrift, frugality, and industry, and with a sense of social obligation. This idea that wealth implied both the favor of God and a duty to be the instrument of divine beneficence is the Puritanism inherited by the Rockefellers, Carnegies, and Fords of later years.

It must not be forgotten that Calvinism is a species of Protestantism, that Protestantism is a species of Christianity, and that the species possesses the characteristics of the genus. Hence the influence of Calvinism carried with it the theistic view of the world, together with the Christian emphasis on the salvation of the individual human soul, an affair so momentous as to constitute, after Creation, the major occupation of the Deity. The human individual, even in his condemnation to eternal punishment, received the personal attention of God. Calvinism carried with it the Christian idea of a universal moral order, and the idea of two Paradises, the original terrestrial Paradise from which man had been expelled, and the future Paradise to which the pious might aspire.

And Calvinism embraced and accentuated the peculiarly individualistic tenets of Protestantism — its recognition of the right of private judgment in the interpretation of Scripture, its emphasis on the personal religious experience, its elimination of ecclesiastical, liturgical, sacramental, and saintly intermediaries between the individual human soul and God.

4

Because of what was found congenial to the American temper in the Puritan-Protestant Christianity of colonial days, the transition to the Eighteenth Century philosophy of the Enlightenment was not abrupt. Americans imbued with Puritanism found in the Enlightenment the same moralism; the same emphasis on the power of the human will; the same conception of property as an index of character and effort, and as embodying the right of a man to the fruits of his own labor; the same interpretation of institutions, political as well as ecclesiastical, as resting on a compact between private parties each of whom was the natural and jealous guardian of his own interests.

Natural rights — to life, liberty, and the pursuit of happiness — and the civil rights embodied in the state constitutions were in keeping with the Protestant conception of the right of the Protestant believer to know for himself the terms of salvation, and to demand his deserts even before the throne of God. The precepts of Puritan morality, and in particular the Golden Rule, were not altered in content when they were called "the Laws of Nature." The dogmatic and other-worldly piety of earlier Protestantism melted through insensible gradations into the mild Deism of the Eighteenth Century in which God became the sanction of duty and the architect of nature. Thomas Paine as well as Jonathan Edwards could find God in the marvels of creation. Benjamin Franklin's practical wisdom and exercises in virtue had been anticipated by Cotton Mather. The State of Nature was scarcely distinguishable from Paradise before the Fall, and both could readily be transferred from the past to the future. Construed in terms of its fundamental ideas the American Revolution was thus a confluence of two British Revolutions, the Puritan Revolution and the Revolution of 1688. It represented not the antithesis but the identity of John Knox and John Locke.

The philosophy of the Declaration of Independence, formulated by Thomas Jefferson not only because he was a skillful draftsman but because he was so completely impregnated with the prevailing opinions of this self-congratulatory age — this age which thought itself so fortunate in its seeing of the light — is the creed solemnly adopted by the nation at its coming of age, and perpetually reaffirmed in all its hours of crisis.

A shrewd observer from abroad [1] has ventured the opinion that America has had no Eighteenth Century, thereby shocking Americans accustomed to believe that America was the child of the Eighteenth Century. The critic was right and the Americans were right. The half-truth could be reversed with the same plausibility. There is a sense in which it is true that *only* America has had an Eighteenth Century. The heart of the paradox lies in the fact that there were two Eighteenth Centuries — the profane and the sacred, the superficial and the profound, the frivolous and the serious. The Eighteenth Century of manners and customs, of worldliness, elegance, and card playing, the Century of George II, George III, and the Whig aristocracy, was not characteristically American. But the underlying principles of this century, its moral, social, and political philosophy, its dreams and forward aspirations, found in America their unique embodiment.

These principles were disseminated in America through many channels: through training in the Common Law and the teachings of Sir Edward Coke; through the political writings of Locke, Sydney, and Milton; through the tradition of Magna Carta, representative government, and the "rights of Englishmen"; through the pulpit oratory of great preachers such as Charles Chauncy, John Wise, and

[1] Alfred North Whitehead.

41

Samuel Davies. These principles — the natural rights of the individual, the grounding of social institutions on an implied contract among individuals, government by the consent of individuals, government for the benefit of individuals, the moral responsibility of the individual, the individual's autonomy through the possession of a reason and conscience of his own, the appeal from the positive law imposed by government to a higher law imposed on each individual by his own faculties — these principles became the charter of Americanism.

5

The difference between the Declaration and the Constitution is commonly overdrawn. They differ not in principle but in priority. The Declaration of Independence contains the premises of the Constitution, whether implicit, or explicitly formulated, as in the Bill of Rights and later amendments. The differences of opinion revealed in the Constitutional Convention and in the development of American constitutional law have to do with the interpretation and application of the philosophy of the Declaration of Independence.

Assuming that government is the creation and the servant of the people, that is, of the aggregate of individuals who live under it, there arises the question of the directness and frequency with which the popular will shall be asserted. Government was thus early associated with tyranny and oppression, and continued to be regarded with suspicion, both by the exponents of the laissez-faire economy and by solitudinarians and near-anarchists such as Thoreau. But when the power of concentrated wealth became a threat to that very freedom of enterprise of which it was the product, Americans began to look to government for protection against the rapacity of their neighbors. No American, of whatever political complexion, would have rejected Thoreau's opinion that "there will never be a really free and enlightened State until the State comes to recognize the individual as a higher and independent power, from which all its own power and authority are derived, and treats him accordingly." [2] But this principle implies that the state must both defer to individuals, and also interfere with them, lest they interfere with one another; and this balancing of the public and the private interest leads to an alternation of emphasis.

American government derives its power from the popular will, which is a composite or resultant of individual wills. But the popular will can be hasty, ignorant, and passionate, or it can be deliberate, wise, and thoughtful; and there is always room for a difference of opinion as to human propensities, and the extent, therefore, to which the people need to be protected against themselves by constitutional procedure, indirection, and delay. America will always have its John Adamses and its Thomas Jeffersons.

America was a federation of states. Was the sovereignty of the Federal government a delegated sovereignty flowing from the sovereignties of the several states, or did it derive its authority directly from the *people* of the United States? Here again there was room for a difference and alternation of emphasis.

American constitutionalism, in short, contains its own dialectic, within the framework of the principles of the Declaration of Independence. But at the same time there has been an unmistakable trend — a line of advance, despite pauses and movements in reverse. In the long run Jefferson has prevailed over Adams; faith over distrust; strong government over weak; the popular will over the rigidities of the system; the rights and the welfare of the people at large over the resistance of the *status quo;* the total nation over the state or region.

[2] "Civil Disobedience," *Miscellanies,* 1894, p. 169.

6

The middle of the Nineteenth Century witnessed an accentuation of that humanitarian impulse which has been a persistent motive in American thought. The anti-slavery movement, the socialist communities and enclaves inspired by Owen and Fourier, concern for the condition of factory workers, temperance reform, the women's rights movement, educational reform, and all the sundry 'isms of the day, expressed one of those periodic outbursts of Christian compassion which mark the course of American history. Horace Mann was an authentic exponent of the scruples of this period when he wrote in 1845:

> By what spirit are our schools animated? Do they cultivate the higher faculties in the nature of childhood, — its conscience, its benevolence, a reverence for whatever is true and sacred; or are they only developing, upon a grander scale, the lower instincts and selfish tendencies of the race, — the desires which prompt men to seek, and the powers which enable them to secure, sensual ends, — wealth, luxury, preferment, — irrespective of the well-being of others? . . . [3]

American individualism is an individualism of the many and not of the one, an inclusive, and not an exclusive, individualism. Each individual, being conceded the right to his own, both in power and in reward, tends to excessive self-assertion, and must therefore be from time to time reminded of the claims of others. He must have his Good Samaritanism excited to balance that self-seeking which needs no exciting.

The economic life of America, its competitiveness and its abundance of opportunity, has added emulation and ambition to native selfishness. Hence the humanitarian reformer, who calls attention to this fact, stresses the equali-

[3] *Report for 1845,* published in the *Common School Journal,* Vol. VIII (1846), pp. 140–1.

tarian implications of the American creed, and speaks in behalf of the exploited or underprivileged. Hence also, the uneasy conscience of the wealthy, such as Andrew Carnegie, who felt impelled to give back in the form of "noble benefactions" what he had taken away in the form of labor, poverty, or frustration. Quoting Thomas Cromwell, he said of the merchants: "If they have a greed of getting, yet in bestowing they are most princely." [4]

7

Benevolence has two sides: the value to the beneficiary in the form of goods received, and the value to the benevolent as a quality of personality. Humanitarianism thus overlapped the movement known as Transcendentalism. Humanitarianism embraced men of affairs who translated benevolence into action and measured it in terms of welfare, while Transcendentalism was confined to an élite who were primarily concerned with their own elevation of mind.

Their primary task was self-education, a task which they could best perform in isolation, in literary self-expression, and in a congenial community of the like-minded. "It is not so important," said Thoreau, "that many should be as good as you, as that there should be some absolute goodness somewhere; for that will leaven the whole lump." "O for a man who is a *man*," he cried; and he felt it his first duty to be, if possible, that man. His first business was with himself: "I came into this world, not chiefly to make this a good place to live in, but to live in it, be it good or bad." [5]

Lowell referred to Emerson as "a Greek head on right Yankee shoulders." [6] Philosophical Transcendentalism, as represented by Emerson and Bronson Alcott, affords a

4 *The Empire of Business*, 1902, p. 225.
5 *Op. cit.*, pp. 139, 141, 146.
6 *Fable for Critics*, 1890, p. 38.

peculiarly pertinent example of the selective emphasis of the American mind. To one who is interested in Americanism the interesting thing is not that Emerson and Alcott should have been influenced by German Romanticism as well as by Plato and by Oriental thought, but what these American thinkers did to these influences before they got through with them. They accepted from Neo-Platonism, from the Coleridgean version of Schelling, and from Brahmanism or from any other available source, the doctrine of a universal indwelling of spirit, or Over-soul apprehended by intuitive reason. But they did not allow the logic of this doctrine to drive them to monism, pantheism, or absolutism. There has never been a more extreme or more defiant champion and exemplar of individualism than Emerson; and the name which Alcott preferred for the gospel which he besought Emerson to join him in proclaiming was the name of "personalism."

Emerson's "Greek head" was his universalism; his gospel of self-reliance formed his "Yankee shoulders." However he may have been drawn toward a metaphysics of the Over-soul, Emerson left no doubt of the individualistic emphasis of his social philosophy. He bids us "remember that no society can ever be so large as one man"; that "the private life of one man shall be a more illustrious monarchy than any kingdom in history." [7] And Alcott was even more emphatic: "Individuals are sacred: creeds, usages, institutions, as they cherish and reverence the individual. The world, the state, the church, the school, are all felons whensoever they violate the sanctity of the private heart." [8] It was the mission of Emerson, Alcott, and their like to humanize, deepen, and spiritualize the individual, and still leave him irreducibly and proudly individual.

[7] "New England Reformers," *Essays*, Second Series, 1883, p. 251; "The American Scholar," *Nature, Addresses and Lectures*, 1890, p. 107.

[8] "Orphic Sayings," *The Dial*, Vol. I (1841), No. 3, p. 359.

8

At the same time that Transcendentalism reigned among men of letters and unofficial sages, another and quite different philosophy won acceptance in the colleges and universities. The Scottish philosophy of Common Sense had been known in the colonies, and Jefferson, among others, had followed its lead in affirming that the self-evident principles of morality were implanted in the original nature of man. But the wide vogue of this school in the Nineteenth Century was due to its link with the Presbyterian ministry, which was usually of Scottish origin and exercised a strong intellectual leadership throughout the country, and to the growing need for a philosophy which could be taught the young without peril to their souls. To meet on their own ground the negations of Biblical criticism and advancing science, such a philosophy must be a secular philosophy, free from sectarian dogma. The Scottish philosophy of Common Sense was at one and the same time moralistic, theistic, and rationalistic. Its chief center was Princeton, beginning with John Witherspoon in 1768 and culminating in James McCosh over a century later. But Yale had its Noah Porter, and many other colleges and universities harbored exponents of the same doctrine.

This philosophy asserted a peculiar claim to acceptance in America. "The Yankees," said McCosh, "have a pretty clear notion of what a thing is, and, if it is of value, they take steps to secure it." [9] In short, according to this most eminent exponent of the Scottish School in America, the American is, by temperament and habit, a practical realist. The individualism of this philosophy was so fundamental and so self-evident that it was scarcely thought necessary to mention it; but if documentation is required,

[9] "What an American Philosophy Should Be," *New Princeton Review*, Vol. I (1886), p. 17.

Thomas Reid, the Scottish founder of the school, can be cited as saying that "a being and an individual being mean the same thing." [10]

9

The Scottish philosophy was easily merged or confused with the Kantian philosophy, which overlapped and eventually replaced it as the form of secular edification which reigned in academic circles.

The influence of Kant, broadly speaking, direct and indirect, was disseminated in America in two waves, the literary movement known as "Transcendentalism," and the strictly philosophical movement, which came to be known as "Post-Kantian Idealism," and was especially identified with the influence of Hegel. This philosophy, in its American manifestations, was notable for its reluctance to sacrifice the individual to the universal. To be guilty of so doing was to violate a deep-seated American scruple. Hence the rise in America of what was called Personal Idealism, which sought to reconcile the rationalism of the Kantians with the moral will of man, and their monism with the pluralism of American democracy. Borden Bowne affords a notable example of this tendency. From his influence sprang a school which adopted the name of "Personalism." It leaped from Boston to Los Angeles — from Boston University to the University of Southern California — created an organ named *The Personalist,* and became the more or less official philosophy of the Methodist ministry, who found it possible to substitute their personal God for the universal Will or Mind of the German philosophers, and John Wesley for Coleridge. These thinkers, together with such eminent thinkers and teachers as Garman of Amherst, Morris and Wenley of Michigan, Watson of Queens, Howison of California, and Royce of Harvard,

[10] *Essays on the Intellectual Powers of Man,* 1785, p. 491.

now became the guardians of the youth, to whom the colleges and universities looked for a non-sectarian and non-dogmatic support of piety against the rising tide of materialism and skepticism.

Of these the most interesting and the most formidable was Josiah Royce, who sprang from the California frontier, conducted his studies in Germany where he was inoculated with literary and philosophical Romanticism, and spent his life compounding the foreign with the native strain. He was profoundly influenced by Schopenhauer, but rejected Schopenhauer's pessimism. He delighted in Hegel's paradoxes and insights, but rejected his historical determinism. He was a Fichtean in his moralism, but followed neither Fichte nor Hegel in their apotheosis of the state. He became known as the chief proponent of "The Absolute," that spiritual frame which holds the world together, and is the infinity implicit in all human finitude; but Royce's Absolute was an American edition of the Absolute. It was no accident that his major work was entitled *The World and the Individual.* Not only was Royce's Absolute itself an individual, but in the end it became a society of finite individuals. Its essence was will, embracing a plurality of wills. Eternity was reconciled with time. Morality consisted essentially in the energetic triumph of good over evil; and the good was loyalty, divisible into a multiplicity of loyalties harmonized through mutual respect and tolerance.

10

At the opening of the present century, when this Americanized Post-Kantian Idealism so dominated the professional philosophical world as to constitute a sort of ruling caste, two powerful thinkers risked the odium of disrepute, and raised the red flag of revolt. It is interesting and characteristically American that the older of these men, William

James, should have sprung from the line of the British School, while John Dewey, his younger and independent ally, had in his earlier years been infected with Hegelianism. Despite the fact that neither of these philosophers ever completely escaped his original bias, they felt themselves to be collaborators, both in what they rejected and in what they affirmed. The course of American philosophy during the last half-century has been largely the result of their joint influence. Together they have brought into vogue that way of philosophizing which affirms the union of thought and action, and is loosely called by the name of "Pragmatism."

Since America and Europe share the same Western philosophical tradition and through their unceasing intercourse form parts of one broad culture, no American philosophy can be said to be purely indigenous. But of Pragmatism it can be said, as it can be said of no other philosophical school, that it was and is distinctively American. James, owing to his sociability, cosmopolitanism, his personal intimacies with European thinkers, and the brilliancy of his style, has been widely read abroad, and especially in France. But the fact remains that Pragmatism, whether of the Jamesian or Deweyan variety, has never taken root outside of the United States. It is worthy of remark that Dewey, who is *facile princeps* among American philosophers today, is in Europe a prophet without honor, save in the sphere of education. This may be taken as negative evidence that Pragmatism is American — not non-American, too American for the alien palate.

That the content of Pragmatism agrees with that general temper of mind which has been ascribed to America needs little argument. James was avowedly and flagrantly a moral individualist; so much so that he can be justly accused of neglecting the human significance of society. He was a fighting moralist, who believed that the issue be-

tween good and evil hung in the balance and could be de-
cided by inspired effort. James's comparative neglect of
the social aspect of human activity was made good by
Dewey; but, although for Dewey individuality is the product of society, it is society's proudest achievement, and
Dewey's entire social philosophy is libertarian and tolerant.
This is notably true of his widely influential educational
philosophy, which in its emphasis on appeal to the interest
of the individual child has been the principal inspiration
of the so-called "progressive" school.

With James and Dewey the "utilitarian" principle, always implicit in American moral philosophy, became explicit. While the principles of right action might still be
disseminated in the form of precepts, and sanctioned by
authority, human or divine, their meaning was found to
lie in their consequences, and their justification in their
meeting human needs and demands. They became rules
for "the pursuit of happiness" — the happiness of all,
achieved by the coöperation of all.

James and Dewey both found the scientific clue to their
philosophies in biology rather than in physics, and looked
to the creative capacity of the human will as the escape
from a necessitarian materialism; but whereas James
stressed the force of the will by which obstacles are overcome, Dewey stresses the intelligence by which they are
circumvented. Dewey, therefore, as compared with James,
is more in line with the American emphasis on organization and technology.

The same difference is reflected in their moral philosophies; James's moralism being more dualistic, more black
and white, more heroic and utopian, while Dewey's is more
piece-meal and opportunistic. Thus while James was ready
to define the goal of moral striving, he was less concerned
with the method of its attainment; while Dewey is so concerned with the method, so unwilling to commit himself to

51

absolutes of any description, as to leave doubt of the end
to which the intelligent and organizing will is to be applied. But both for James and for Dewey the moral will is
the temporal and limited will of man, sprung from nature,
and operating in the natural environment. They know no
other — no transcendent will, no absolute will, no eternal
will, no hypothetical will designed to satisfy the requirements of a speculative metaphysics.

11

Pragmatism, despite its wide vogue in America, has
never attained the high respectability once enjoyed by
Protestant-Puritanism, by the Scottish School, and by Post-
Kantian Idealism. It is a philosophy which does not readily
lend itself to authority, to orthodoxy, or to edification. The
same can be said of the divers schools for which Pragmatism
prepared the way. The lines of Idealism having been
broken, various philosophies of less august repute, and
showing little reverence for the "Great Tradition," poured
through the breach; being esteemed by the Idealists very
much as the New Deal is esteemed by the National Association of Manufacturers.

There thus sprang into being in the early decades of the
present century a number of movements, having at most a
sort of cousinship more or less removed. Their diversity
was marked by a tendency which appears to be peculiarly
American, the tendency, namely, to publish coöperative
studies, in which the authors professed a bond of doctrinal
agreement. These groups were not discipleships of a
master, but rather philosophical parties, created partly for
polemical or propagandist purposes, partly in order that
their members might enjoy agreement (or the illusion of
agreement), and discuss their lesser differences within its
framework.

The first of these groups called itself "The New Realism," [11] and was composed of thinkers who rejected the idealism of Idealism — its subjectivism, or reduction of the object of knowledge to the knowing mind — while at the same time affirming that the independent real was brought immediately before the mind in the act of knowledge. This group was followed by the "Critical Realists," [12] who also rejected subjective idealism, but returned to something like the older dualism; holding the real objects of knowledge, such as bodies, to be accessible only by inference, being screened from the knowing mind by its own states, or by so-called "essences" which were neither physical nor mental.

A later wave of European influence to inundate American philosophy was "Logical Positivism," derived from the Austrian philosophical physicist, Ernst Mach. This philosophy allowed its votaries to enjoy in the field of symbolic logic the immunities and the expertness of a specialized and highly technical branch of inquiry, and so to feel themselves members of the intellectual caste of exact science. But while its contributions to the foundations of mathematics and to scientific methodology have been notable, taken as a total philosophy it has tended to find common ground with Pragmatism, Realism, Materialism, or some other of the older schools. Meanwhile, the Idealists have rallied and published *their* coöperative volume under the title of "Contemporary Idealism"; [13] and Pragmatism, under new names, such as "Operationalism," "Instrumentalism," and "Contextualism," has continued to insist on the rôle of thought as a practical dealing with "concrete situations."

It is significant that the last coöperative publishing ven-

11 Title of volume published in 1912.
12 *Essays in Critical Realism,* 1920.
13 Published in 1932.

ture among American philosophers should have been entitled "Naturalism and the Human Spirit." [14] Naturalism,
pro or con, has recently become the broadest controversial
issue in American philosophy. While the meaning of the
term "naturalism" is by no means clear, its use suggests a
realignment of forces.

There are, in fact, two Naturalisms, and therefore two
controversies. In the older and extremer sense, Naturalism
takes its cue from Newtonian physics: the real is ponder-
able matter, and the fundamental explanation of events is
to be found in the laws of mechanics. Against this view are
arrayed all philosophies which insist that life and mind
have irreducible claims of their own. These philosophies
appeal to biology, psychology, or the social sciences against
physics; or find support in the newer developments of
physics itself.

In a newer and less extreme sense Naturalism means that
life and mind, while irreducible to matter and mechanism,
have nevertheless emerged from the temporal stream and
dwell on the same plane with physical nature. This broader
Naturalism embraces Bergson, James, Dewey, and other
thinkers who call themselves "empirical idealists" or "spir-
itualists," in the French sense of that term. The opponent
of this Naturalism is Post-Kantian Idealism, chastened, but
unrepentant. Its votaries affirm, as against all Naturalisms,
whether broad or narrow, that the whole temporal process,
physical nature and human history alike, are subordinate,
in the order of being and explanation, to a transcendent,
or eternal, principle, which is revealed to man, in advance
of experience, by his intellectual and moral faculties.

During the last two decades American philosophers have
been much preoccupied with "theory of value"; and here
the most fundamental cleavage of doctrine is that between
Naturalism (in the broader sense) and Post-Kantian Ideal-

[14] Published in 1944.

ism. The Naturalists, however differing among themselves, agree in relating value to the actual desires and interests of men; so that value takes its place in the world at the point where life, or some more or less advanced form of human life, emerges from the temporal stream. For Idealism, on the other hand, value is primordial, being a sort of lodestar or magnetic pole which attracts and directs the human will.

In all this diversity and opposition of views there is no disparagement of the individual, whether as moral agent or as thinker — no absolutism, no mystical self-surrender and dissolution, no tragic futility, no subjection of man to institutions, no pessimism, no misanthropy, but a pervasive individualism, in the sense which is the opposite of all these things. American philosophy has resisted every form of fatalism, whether of the pantheistic right or the materialistic left, and has favored that view of the world which most closely coincides with the outlook of hopeful action — that outlook which takes things as they are in order to make them better.

Despite, or perhaps because of, the clash of doctrines, American philosophy tends to moderation. Its different ideas rub against one another, after the manner of gregarious Americans. Friction dulls the sharp edges of difference and works against intellectual obsession or monomania. There are very few American thinkers who do not have more than one idea. American philosophy does not tend to fanaticism, to doctrinaire rigidity, to pontifical utterance, or, and this may be held to be a weakness, to system-building. It shrinks from extremes, whether skeptical or speculative. This disposition is connected with that tendency to hospitality and eclecticism which has already been remarked; and it may account for America's comparative lack of philosophical daring and originality — its producing many busy thinkers rather than a few sages, prophets and revolutionaries. It is symbolized not by ivory towers but by union railway stations, or by sky-scrapers which accommodate a throng of occupants, engaged in diverse enterprises whose offices are connected by elevators, telephones, and public address systems.

This American disposition to combine and organize the efforts of individuals has manifested itself in recent years in the demand that philosophers shall deal with life and with current issues, and shall collaborate with their colleagues in other fields. "Orientation" courses, courses in the humanities, courses in "general education," courses in the "philosophy of" this or that in which the traditional curricular boundaries are broken down, are the order of the day in the American liberal arts colleges. The studies and writings of American philosophers are largely concerned with aesthetics and criticism, with social and economic problems, with scientific methodology, and other border-line subjects. This trend has many causes; the effort of the philosophers to obtain a wider hearing, the educational reaction against excessive specialization, the recognition that in an age when ideologies are at war the philosopher has a peculiar responsibility for their creation or criticism. But, whatever its causes, this demand that the philosopher shall descend to earth, come out of his closet, and mingle with his fellows on the open plane of social intercourse, finds a ready response among Americans — whose Americanism disposes them to get together and work together.

12

This summary of American philosophy is guilty of notable omissions. Catholic thought adheres so rigidly to the teachings of Thomas Aquinas as to leave little room for American variations. Two eminent philosophers, George Santayana and Charles Peirce, fail to satisfy the formula, and serve to prove (or disprove) the rule by their exceptionality. They must be considered as un-American, though scarcely subversive. A third, Alfred North Whitehead, can scarcely be reckoned as an American for reasons of origin.

Santayana has excluded himself. He found the American environment repellent, and has said so; and what he found repellent is precisely that which has here been defined as American — its moral earnestness, its voluntarism, its disrespect for authority and historic institutions, its belief in progress through effort and organization. Together with James he rejected Royce, only in the end to reject James as well. So that Santayana, despite his vogue as a master of style, and despite his partial acceptance of Pragmatism and his passing participation in the group movement of the Critical Realists, remains tangential. His Olympian escapism, his delicately mocking attitude to man's effort to better himself and his world, have proved as unacceptable to Americans as their ways to him: which is not to be taken as implying disparagement.

Charles Peirce stands like a lonely peak, its altitude increasing with distance. It would put too much strain upon its meaning to embrace him within the Americanism which has here been expounded. He explicitly rejected individualism, and he is himself the best authority that can be cited on the subject. He was an isolated figure, a philosopher's philosopher, who belonged to no school, drew from the philosophical classics, from science, and from his own original genius, and had little commerce, personal or intellectual, with his contemporary environment. He became the imputed father of Pragmatism but refused the, to him, doubtful honor. His evolutionary Naturalism won him posthumous support among followers of Dewey. But he cannot be classified.

Whitehead's experience was very different. Although America cannot claim to have produced him, America harbored, nourished him, and made him happy. His many-sided and tentative manner of philosophizing, his intellectual tolerance, his suspicion of systems, his understanding of contemporary science, his naturalism, his realism, his personal involvement in the two world wars and devotion to the cause of the Allies, his agreement with liberal social and economic trends both in Britain and in America, his admiration of William James above all American philosophers, his empirical sense of a universe rich in undisclosed possibilities, his setting of wisdom above learning, his hailing the promise of youth — all of these traits of character and of mind enabled him to ally himself with, and take his place among, American philosophers, at the same time that he remained an expression of English culture and tradition.

13

American thought, like that of every modern society, has reflected the reigning concepts and the new advances of natural science; America, in fact, has been peculiarly receptive to such advances. "Popular science" has a wide reading public; and scientific discoveries are considered "news"; the press has its "science reporters."

Until the middle of the Nineteenth Century the influence of science in America was identified with the illustrious name of Isaac Newton, who was happily a physicist, a theist, and a man of the Enlightenment. As Newton was interpreted in his own age, the exactness of nature's laws testified to the Creator's reason, their discovery testified to the power of human reason, and the generalization of the force of gravitation supported the belief in an original First Cause.

It was the extension of natural science to man — first to his body, and then to his soul — that threatened the foundations of traditional piety. This tendency was transplanted to America during the Revolutionary Period through the influence of Joseph Priestley, who had migrated from England; and it appears in the writings of Cadwallader Colden, Benjamin Rush, and other founders of American medical science whose observations led them to emphasize the intimate dependence of man's higher faculties on bodily conditions. Franklin and Jefferson, having felt this influence in America, found a philosophical bond with the Encyclopaedists and other intellectual precursors of the French Revolution.

This reduction of man to terms of physical nature received a powerful reënforcement in America as well as in Europe through the doctrines of evolution and the conservation of energy — both of which were promulgated about 1860. Meanwhile, from about 1840, America had felt the influence of the Positivistic School of Auguste Comte, continued by John Stuart Mill, and later resumed and modernized by the Austrian School of Ernst Mach.

These successive waves of the scientific philosophy revealed the peculiar American emphasis. Once natural science had ceased to be the handmaid of theology it became the instrument of man's control of his physical environment and a guarantee of material progress. The inventive and technological emphasis of Benjamin Franklin is significant and symbolic. The popularity of the doctrine of evolution in America, exemplified by the vogue of Herbert Spencer and his American disciple, John Fiske, was due to its seeming agreement with the idea that nature as well as history tended to the increase of human happiness. The pessimistic implications of science — its denial of God and immortality, its representation of the environment as hostile, or at best indifferent, to the moral will — created in America as elsewhere a cult of disillusionment, and was associated with a "naturalistic" and "realistic" movement in literature; but American illusions, while sobered, were never seriously undermined. The war between science and religion, proclaimed towards the end of the Nineteenth Century, ended in a stalemate, or a settlement which left religion intact though in possession of a reduced domain.

Natural science is congenial to the American temper of mind because it discloses that realm of existence which lies on the same plane as human action — that spatio-temporal-causal nexus within which mortal man lives out his three-score years and ten, and within which men make their own history and refashion their environment. Americans see in the method of science a technique for the utilization of the forces of physical nature. Nature is at one and the same time a source of power and a plastic medium in which power is exercised. Margaret Mead has contrasted the British view of the world as an environment to which man is compelled to adapt himself, with the American view of the world "as man-controlled, a vast malleable space on which one builds what one wishes, from blueprints one has drawn, and, when dissatisfied, simply tears the structure down and starts anew." [15]

The disillusionment with science itself, which in the present century has spread throughout the world, has tended in America to be confined to physical science, and to be accompanied by the belief that through its extension to man and society science can find a way not only of controlling nature but of controlling the controls so that they shall be directed to good uses.

14

The philosophical premises laid down in the Seventeenth and Eighteenth Centuries have continued to deter-

[15] *Transactions of the New York Academy of Sciences,* Series II, Vol. 9 (1947), pp. 141-2.

mine the later developments of the social sciences in America. There *have been* developments, which have reflected currents of thought in the world at large and the changing conditions of American life, but new interpretations and applications have proved the persistence of the premises themselves.

Reviewing the influence of Francis Lieber, Theodore Woolsey, and John W. Burgess in the later decades of the Nineteenth Century, C. E. Merriam said:

> It appears that recent political theory shows a decided tendency away from many doctrines that were held by the men of 1776. The same forces that have led to the general abandonment of the individualistic philosophy of the eighteenth century by political scientists elsewhere have been at work here and with the same result. The Revolutionary doctrines of an original state of nature, natural rights, the social contract, the idea that the function of government is limited to the protection of person and property, — none of these finds wide acceptance among the leaders of political science.[16]

This wave of thought has rolled over the American mind and left its underlying political convictions intact. The significant fact is not the spread from Germanic sources of the idea that the state is an organic and historic entity, rather than an artefact created by compact; or that this idea should have suited the nationalistic emphasis of the period succeeding the Civil War. The significant fact is that in the end the compact theory was not abandoned, but clarified and reaffirmed in terms closer to its original meaning than the terms employed by its critics. For this theory has always referred to the *ground* of the state, and not to its genesis — to its "why," and not to its "how" or "when." The earlier exponents of the compact theory were ignorant

[16] *History of American Political Theories*, 1920, p. 332. The author admits that "the political scientists are more agreed upon [these points] than is the general public." *Ibid.*, p. 311.

or careless of history, and were thus vulnerable to later advances in historical learning. But historical criticism was beside the point, and did not discredit the idea that the *justification* of the state lies in its being a joint enterprise agreed on, whether explicitly or tacitly, by the several individuals who live under it and hope severally to profit by it. Americans still feel that whatever the accidents of its origin, their government is theirs, to make, unmake, or modify as may appear best to suit their interests.

Similarly, in a period when the authority of the Federal Government had been asserted and preserved by a bloody civil war, the idea of absolute sovereignty — a sovereignty proceeding from above, and to which individuals, classes, and sections should yield obedience, found ready acceptance. But the theory of the founding fathers cut deeper. It no doubt failed sufficiently to recognize that if a government is to fulfil its function it must *govern,* that is, command obedience; but this needed emphasis proved quite consistent with the idea that the justification of such a compelling authority comes back in the end to an agreement among the governed that they need to be governed, and to their consequent willingness to make the necessary sacrifices of liberty.

Similarly, the historical-organic school of jurisprudence has spoken and been heard with profit in America, but to Americans it does not speak the last word. American legal thought does not deny that law has historical causes, and that it is interwoven with the social conditions of time and place. But the idea which has come to dominate American law-making and judicial decisions is that law is useful in the resolving of conflicts of interest, in the ordering of human affairs, and in the promotion of welfare.

The important opinions in which is recorded the history of American constitutional law reveal two unmistakable characteristics. The first is the appeal to the rights embodied in the Declaration of Independence; the second is the acceptance of the standard of welfare: in other words, the principle of individual liberty, and the principle of individual happiness — both liberty and happiness being conceived in equalitarian terms. And these two principles, despite their momentary conflict, are recognized as fundamentally in accord with one another. For the pursuit of happiness is an individual right; and the general happiness is the standard by which rights are interpreted and limited.[17]

The worship of the Constitution in America is not due to any legalistic propensity — any regard for the existing legal system as such — but to the fact that the Constitution embodies the principles of the Declaration of Independence. There is still an appeal from the positive law to "the higher law"; which is less frequently referred to as "natural law" or "the law of God," but which still signifies the ultimate moral premises by which the positive law is justified. The sanction of law is not the law itself, or the command of the state, but the principles of individual right and good which commend themselves to the reason and conscience of mankind.

Economic thought in America has moved steadily away from an academic classicism in the direction of emphasis on concrete problems of industrial or agricultural production, employment, labor relations, national income, and standards of living. Laissez-faire capitalism has been called upon to deliver that general good which it has always promised, but which has heretofore been taken largely on faith. The humanitarian purpose of economy has become more explicit. This trend has made itself felt not only through social reformers such as Jane Addams, through

[17] Cf. Field's opinion in the Slaughterhouse case, *111 U.S.* 755, 760 (1884); Holmes in Abrams v. U.S., *250 U.S.* 616 (1919); Brandeis in Whitney v. California, *274 U.S.* 357 (1927).

the labor movement, and through the Christian churches, but through the insistence of economists themselves, such as Richard T. Ely, that economics is essentially a moral science, dedicated to the purpose of social beneficence.[18] While "free enterprise" is still a phrase to conjure with, there has been a growing insistence that it shall be in fact both free and enterprising, and that its uses shall outweigh its abuses.

When, in 1936, Franklin Roosevelt uttered the following words, he was speaking not for a party, or from a merely personal conviction, but as the exponent of Americanism brought up to date and looking toward the future:

> Private enterprise . . . became too private. It became privileged enterprise, not free enterprise. . . . They [the economic royalists] granted that the Government could protect the citizen in his right to vote, but they denied that the Government could do anything to protect the citizen in his right to work and his right to live. . . . Better the occasional faults of a Government that lives in a spirit of charity than the consistent omissions of a Government frozen in the ice of its own indifference. . . . Each one of us has learned the glories of independence. Let each one of us learn the glories of interdependence.[19]

The general trend of American social philosophy can be summarized as a shift in the sanctions and the evidence by which the same moral principles are justified. The principles are those which have been stated in terms of collective individualism: the valid claim of all members of society to share in the control of its institutions and the enjoyment of their benefits; and the purpose through improved organization to make the individual's control more effective, and his share of its benefits more abundant.

[18] Cf. Richard T. Ely's *Social Aspects of Christianity and Other Essays,* 1889.
[19] *The Public Papers and Addresses of Franklin Delano Roosevelt,* 1938, Vol. V, pp. 233, 233-4, 235, 601.

15

To distil the peculiar flavor of American thought, it would be necessary to attempt a critical estimate of American criticism as well as of American literature; or of the two as united in a literature which is both creative and critical.

The central theme of the American literature of protest and disillusionment, embracing poets and fiction-writers of great diversity from Melville and Poe down to Theodore Dreiser, Sinclair Lewis and William Faulkner, has been the American tendency to wishful thinking. What is demanded is not a revision of American ideals, but a less flattering appraisal of achievement. Attention has been called to the immense gap between profession and action, or between the goal and the distance already traveled. The object of hope and the object of doubt, or even despair, is the same object. Utopia is not denied, but postponed, or removed to an infinitely distant future. Edwin Markham having described "The Man with the Hoe" as "stolid and stunned, a brother to the ox," then asked,

> Is this the Thing the Lord God made and gave
> To have dominion over sea and land? [20]

Nothing was further from the poet's thoughts than to deny the ideal dignity of man or his claim to dominion.

Broadly speaking, the "realists" who wrote at the close of the Nineteenth Century did not proclaim a gospel of despair, but a gospel of courage — courage to face the facts. They were not destroyers of Americanism, but of complacency and squeamishness. To use William James's expression, their idealism was of the "tough-minded," rather than the "tender-minded," variety. In keeping with the growing influence of science they were prepared to assume the in-

[20] *The Man with the Hoe, and Other Poems,* 1900, p. 2.

difference or even hostility of nature. Like Melville they were aware of men's disposition to read out of nature what their hopes have already read into it:

> Say what some poets will, Nature is not so much her own ever-cunning sweet interpreter, as the mere supplier of that conniving alphabet, whereby selecting and combining as he pleases, each man reads his own peculiar lesson according to his own peculiar mind and mood.[21]

American criticism has fearlessly acknowledged the unsavory aspects of American life — its bitterness, its brutalities, and its indignities. It has found good not in retreat from the American scene but in the very flavor of its crudeness. As Howells said:

> We are really a mixture of the plebeian ingredients of the whole world; but that is not bad; our vulgarity consists in trying to ignore "the worth of the vulgar," in believing that the superfine is better.[22]

This is the broad tendency of American critical literature — not impiety, but repentance and fresh resolve. America has no doubt had its Henry Jamesian nostalgias for the riper and more static culture of Europe, its Walt Whitmanesque moods of promiscuous acceptance, its moods of escapism or defeatism, as in Thoreau and Poe. American writers and critics have sometimes found compensation in despising those values of American life which they have personally failed to realize. But Van Wyck Brooks is on the wrong track when he condemns America for its lack of constructive criticism, as when he says that Americans have not known "the difference between the trap-drum and the lyre and lute, or between the Valley of Democracy and the Kingdom of Heaven." [23] Americans

[21] *Pierre,* 1923, p. 476.
[22] W. D. Howells, "Breaking New Ground," in his *Criticism and Fiction,* 1891, p. 81.
[23] "The Critical Movement," in *Sketches in Criticism,* 1932, p. 19.

have known the difference. They simply have not accepted this writer's exaltation of the lyre and lute, but have thought more highly than he of the trap-drums of collective human achievement; they have refused to lower democracy to the valley, but have placed it on the heights close to the Kingdom of Heaven.

16

Van Wyck Brooks has also said of Americans that "we have had no candid friends of our own race, no 'national conscience,' in short." [24] Nothing could be further from the truth: America fairly bristles with conscience. There is no nation on earth, no nation in history, that has had a more tenacious creed. What is characteristically American is not slavery, segregation, racial prejudice, exploitation, ruthlessness, materialism, but the self-reproach, the inner tensions and conflicts, which these evils generate. They are not accepted passively, because Americans believe that evils can be eradicated by the organization and effort of the human will. The American creed is a faith, stronger than recurrent doubts.

This individualistic and humanitarian creed, this faith in the power of the implemented moral will, received its classic statement in the Declaration of Independence. It was there stated in universal terms so that it remains applicable to changed conditions and to more extended human relationships. In proportion as America achieved a national consciousness this creed and this faith became a national conscience. In his famous Cooper Union speech of 1860, Lincoln said that the South asked not only that slavery be tolerated, but that it be approved; and this, he insisted, Americans cannot do, for the simple reason that "slavery is wrong." By the same token Americans believe

[24] *Op. cit.*, p. 13.

in their hearts that discrimination against the emancipated slave is wrong; and so long as nothing is done about it, America must suffer a sense of shame which can be relieved only when something *is* done about it. And the North will suffer from this sense of shame, and seek to do something about it, because the American conscience is national and not sectional. By the same token the South suffers for the sins of the North, and all sections for the sins of all sections, when they violate the common national creed.

Adherence to this creed is the condition of national morale. It is eloquently, or at least loudly, professed by candidates for office. For better or for worse, it has inspired, or been invoked to justify, the successive "movements" of American history, the Westward movement, the Jacksonian rising of the common man, anti-slavery, free-soil, anti-imperialism, the "New Freedom," the "Square Deal," the "New Deal," the Labor Movement, "Rugged Individualism," "Free Enterprise," the United Nations, Anti-Communism. Even our xenophobias, our isolationisms, and our Know-Nothingisms, have found support in the perversions and distortions of this creed. American psychoses, as diagnosed by critics of the psychoanalytical school, are attributed to its repressive effects. The Presidents of acknowledged greatness — Washington, Jefferson, Jackson, Lincoln, Theodore Roosevelt, Wilson, and Franklin Roosevelt — have spoken and acted in the name of this same creed, and sought to lead the country in the direction of its requirements.

The American balance between the complacent and the despairing conscience, the strengthening of resolve through conviction of sin, was fitly expressed in the following lines of William Vaughn Moody:

> Are we the eagle nation Milton saw
> Mewing its mighty youth,
> Soon to possess the mountain winds of truth,

And be a swift familiar of the sun
Where aye before God's face his trumpets run?
Or have we but the talons and the maw,
And for the abject likeness of our heart
Shall some less lordly bird be set apart? —
Some gross-billed wader where the swamps are fat? . . .
Ah, no!
We have not fallen so.
We are our fathers' sons: let those who lead us know! [25]

[25] *An Ode in Time of Hesitation.*

III

William James and
American Individualism

1

THE MOST PERFECT philosophical expression of American individualism is to be found in the thought and personal characteristics of William James. He was a restless and mobile man, who spent much time abroad, spoke and read several languages, was linked by personal affection with philosophers of many lands, and drew many of his ideas from European sources. Nevertheless, he was profoundly in sympathy with American democratic institutions, loved the American landscape with all its frontier crudities and untamed wildness, and identified himself unreservedly with the zestful and sanguine spirit of American life. He was not an American nationalist, and vigorously repudiated American imperialism; not because he was un-American, but because he felt that both nationalism and imperialism were betrayals of a better form of success to which America was dedicated.

It is characteristic of James, in other words, that while he extended the range of his sympathies he never lost the center of his attachment — to family, to home, and to country. He spent his life accumulating friends, but the new did not displace the old. He could say of America, "I believe . . . ours is eventually the bigger destiny"; and add, quoting his brother Henry, "thank God for a world that holds so rich an England, so rare an Italy." [1] He felt the thinness and poverty of American culture, and fell in love with each European country which he visited, but was never unfaithful at heart. In 1901 when, owing to the interruption of his Gifford Lectures by illness, James had been in Europe for nearly two years, he wrote:

> I long to steep myself in America again and let the broken rootlets make new adhesions to the native soil. A man coquetting with too many countries is as bad as a bigamist, and loses his soul altogether. [2]

2

To discuss James and American individualism is at one and the same time to clarify three topics, James, American, and *individualism*. For individualism has many distinct meanings, which James illustrates, and which are implicit in that vaguer and more generalized meaning which has in earlier chapters been attributed to America.

The root-meaning of individualism arises from that distinction in human thought which is commonly expressed among philosophers as the distinction between the "universal" and the "particular." However this distinction may be interpreted, there is no escaping it. The Platonic tradition exalts the universal — as the metaphysical essence, and the object of true knowledge; debasing the particular to the status of non-being, irrationality, or appearance. The so-called "nominalistic" tradition, on the other hand, exalts the particular, as the really existent, and as final evidence of certifiable fact; while debasing the universal to the rôle of a word or a tool of thought. And there are various compromises between these two extreme views. Individualism inclines to the second view.

[1] R. B. Perry, *Thought and Character of William James, Briefer Version*, 1948, p. 248.
[2] *Ibid.*, p. 249.

But there are further distinctions which it is essential to note. In modern times it is customary to distinguish between two kinds of universals — the "abstract" and the "concrete." Thus there are two human universals, the abstract character MAN, of which all particular men are instances; and the concrete totality of mankind, of which all particular men are members. The second meaning assumes special importance when the members of the totality are so interrelated that the totality itself possesses significant characteristics which the members taken severally do not possess. The totality then becomes a "whole," like an army or an institution, while the members become its "parts"; and in proportion as the characteristics of the parts are derived from the whole, the latter is said to be "organic." Thus an organic human society, if there were such, would have a double universality: its members would be instances of the abstract universal MAN; and they would compose a whole, or concrete universal, from which they would borrow what was most important about them.

Although it would be pedantic in the present context to insist on a rigid use of terms, it should be kept in mind, then, that the term "particular" may mean particular instance of an abstract universal, or particular part of a more or less organic whole; or it may mean both, whether explicitly or ambiguously.

The terms particular and individual may be used synonymously, and applied to any subject-matter, as when one refers to a particular or individual pea in a pod. But the term "individual" is commonly used to mean a particular of a specific universal, namely, man. Thus if one were to say that there were several hundred individuals in an auditorium, one would be taken to refer not to the seats, but to their occupants. Because the term "individual" is used to mean a particular *man* it suggests the possession both of general human attributes and of the human peculiarities

72

which distinguish one particular man from another — all the associations of the human proper name, of the singular personal pronoun, and of the particularizing attitudes and relations among the personal members of society. The term "individuality," in short, is invested with all the richness of meaning which distinguishes human from other particularities.

These, then, are the preliminary distinctions which it is well to have in mind in exploring the individualism of William James: the particular instance as distinguished from the abstract universal; the particular member or part as distinguished from the whole; the particular human instance and human member or part, as distinguished respectively from the abstract universal MAN, and from the human whole or social group. The more general particularism appears in James's metaphysics and theory of knowledge; the more limited human particularism in his psychology, and in his moral, social, and religious philosophy.

3

First, then, omitting the limiting adjective "human," and taking "individual" to mean the same as particular of any kind, James's individualism places him metaphysically on the side of particulars — as opposed both to abstract universals and to indivisible wholes. The following paragraphs are taken from notes made during the period when he was making preliminary sketches of his final metaphysical position, which he here designated as "empiricism" or "pluralism":

> By empiricism I mean the tendency which lays most stress on the part, the element, the individual, treats the whole as a collection, and calls the universal an abstraction.
> This picture of the irremediably pluralistic evolution of things, achieving unity by experimental methods, and getting

it in different shapes and degrees, and in general only as a last result, is what has made me give to my volume the title of "The Many and the One."

How, on the supposition that the manyness of things precedes their unity, does any unity come into being at all? And of all the different kinds of unity which the universe of our experience encloses, which is the essential kind, after the pattern of which we may imagine the other kinds to be constructed? The essential kind, in my view . . . is the continuity, the absolute nextness of one part to another, which we find in the minutest portions of our inner experience.[3]

It is clear from these passages that James did not allow his particularism to become an obsession. He was too good a philosopher for that. Wholeness is just as palpable a fact as plurality and diversity. His intent was not to deny wholes, but to affirm the priority of the parts to the whole, and to describe the *kind of whole* which is secondary to its parts. This kind of whole he found in the continuity of the immediate conscious stream, in which particulars flow into one another, and in which wholes emerge out of the togetherness and accretion of particulars. Thus we find James using and extending a set of terms which he had stressed in his psychology in the early 80's: "nextness," "transitiveness," "co-terminousness," "osmosis," "confluence." "The essence of my contention," he said,

is that in a world in which connections are not logically necessary, they may nevertheless adventitiously *"come."* Series of independent origin and purpose may inosculate by "chance-encounter," and thereafter mingle their causalities, and combine their effects.[4]

James would, perhaps, have accepted the analogy of the jazz orchestra, in which the total effect, instead of being premeditated and written in the score, is improvised by the

---

[3] R. B. Perry, *Thought and Character of William James,* 1935, Vol. II, pp. 379–80.

[4] *Op. cit.,* Vol. II, p. 382.

players as they go along; each in turn adding something new of his own accord, but at the same time catching up what has gone before and rounding it into a new whole.

As James's particularism did not lead him to *ignore* wholeness and unity, but rather to give a particularistic account of them, so his particularism led him to a particularistic account of abstract universals. In the first place, they are abstractions *from* particulars. Abstraction is *ex*traction; and if the universals were not in the concrete particulars they could not be extracted. Being abstracted they can then be examined by themselves, as in mathematics. But they should not be said to exist, *in abstracto*. To understand what they really are, the act of abstraction must be reversed; the skeleton must be reinvested with its original flesh. Furthermore, abstraction itself is a particular act. How do universals come to be abstracted? Because, says James, they serve as instruments of classification and control employed by individuals.

In short, particularity says the last word, either in terms of the sensory experience in which abstract universals lie embedded, or in terms of the practical experience by which they are selected and employed for the guidance of action. Abstract universals are deeply rooted in particulars: the full particularity of the *not-yet-abstracted,* to which their origin can be ultimately traced; and the particularity of the abstracting itself, from which they derive their practical or theoretical usefulness.

4

James's theory of knowledge shows a similar emphasis on the particular. The type of whole which James considers to be most fundamental, whether in the aboriginal reality or in the moral organization of society, is the whole which is to be *explained* in terms of its parts. In his Pragmatism, furthermore, the meaning and the truth of ideas are construed in terms of their prospective reference to particulars. Two ideas are different when and only when they *make* a difference: that is, when their difference can be translated into terms of perception or action:

> The meaning of any proposition can always be brought down to some particular consequence in our future practical experience, whether passive or active . . . the point lying rather in the fact that the experience must be particular than in the fact that it must be active.[5]

Then, when ideas are affirmed in belief or judgment, their truth lies in their verification by particular experience. Here James is in agreement with the method of experimental science, which requires that all theories, although *framed* in terms of logic and mathematics, shall be accepted only when their deduced sensory predictions are fulfilled. The difference between James's broader empiricism and the stricter techniques of the natural sciences lies in James's refusal to limit verification to measurable sense-data, precisely localizable in space and time. Ideas may be verified in terms of *any* experience, provided only it is accessible to the knowing mind, and is particular.

5

James's psychological, social, moral, and religious individualisms were corollaries of the basic individualism of his metaphysics and theory of knowledge. This he repeatedly affirmed; as, for example, in a note in which he likened the novel event, by which things change without losing their identity, to a graft:

> A graft is an additive to a tree. Nobody can contend that it is essential. Yet it combines harmoniously, replaces another branch that would have come, or another scion that

[5] James, *Meaning of Truth*, 1909, p. 210.

might equally well have been grafted, and redefines the "whole tree. . . ."

The *graft*-theory . . . means anarchy in the good sense. It means *individualism, personalism:* that the prototype of reality is the *here* and *now* . . . that order is being *won*, — incidentally reaped; that the more universal is the more abstract; that the smaller and more intimate is the truer, — the man more than the home, the home more than the state or the church. . . . It means tolerance and respect. It means democracy as against systems which crush the individual. . . . It means hero-worship and leadership. It means the vital and the growing as against the fossilized and fixed, in science, art, religion, custom, government. It means faith and help; in morals, obligation respondent to demand.[6]

James's psychology was dynamic and voluntaristic. The *human* particular, the individual *man* is, according to James, a particularity of will. In his *Principles of Psychology* James had identified will with the effort or strain of attention by which an idea takes possession of the field of consciousness, and then, in accordance with the ideo-motor or impulsive theory of mind, is automatically translated into action. "The essential achievement of the will, in short, when it is most 'voluntary,' is to ATTEND to a difficult object and hold it fast before the mind." [7]

Apart from this emphasis on the effort or fiat of the will, James also uses the term to express the whole range of interest, from elementary impulses and instincts through the more elaborate emotions and sentiments, to conscious preferences and deliberate choices. The human individual's individuality lies in his peculiar bias — he becomes individual by virtue of what he in particular is for and against.

James's idea of will distinguishes his view profoundly from that of the most famous representatives of the volun-

6 R. B. Perry, *Thought and Character of William James*, 1935, Vol. II, p. 383.

7 James, *Principles of Psychology*, 1890, Vol. II, p. 561.

taristic school. For Schopenhauer the multiplicity of wills is mere appearance — a mere phenomenon relative to the human understanding. There is in reality only one will. For Schopenhauer, furthermore, will is essentially self-defeating and insatiable — a perpetual renewal of craving, and therefore of misery. Hence philosophy, according to Schopenhauer, leads to a theoretic denial of individuality, and morals to a pessimistic cultivation of will-lessness. On both counts James's view is the precise opposite of Schopenhauer's — affirming a real multiplicity of wills, each confident, and rightly confident, of positive achievement.

James's identification of human particularity with will was symmetrical. The human individual is essentially will, and will is essentially individual. In his voluntaristic interpretation of man, James rejected the leveling down of human nature to merely mechanistic or physico-chemical terms; but he also rejected with equal emphasis the leveling up of human nature to terms of thought and intellectual contemplation. He took them both to be dogmatisms — the dogmatism of materialism and the dogma of rationalism. He took man as he found him — a being of appetite and passion, but also, within limits, an intelligent being, whose intellect serves his will, with varying degrees of enlightenment. Thinking and inquiry are rooted in practice and are themselves a kind of practice. Truth ministers to success and is itself a kind of success; to err is to fail, or to cause failure.

In his individualistic interpretation of will James rejected all of those philosophies, springing for the most part from Romanticism and Transcendentalism, which proclaimed a Common Will, or Universal Will, or Absolute Will, or National Will, or Will of the State — in short, a corporate will. He thought of will in terms of those actual wills which are open to observation, and which fall within the domain of natural science. It is of the essence of will, so regarded, that there should be many wills, lying on the same plane of intercourse and interaction, rather than one Over-all Will, occupying a privileged position.

6

The will of the human individual is free. James fought for the cause of freedom on many fronts. Mechanistic necessity he rejected as a materialistic dogma. His doctrine of the relation of whole and parts liberated the parts from the control of the whole; and permitted him to believe in the occurrence of genuinely novel events — of particular events which are beginnings, and not predetermined unfoldings of an irrevocable past, or necessary implications of an enveloping system.

It is significant that the essay on "The Dilemma of Determinism," which is James's most famous and most complete discussion of the topic of freedom, should concern itself mainly with the human individual's freedom not from physical forces but from a higher human or divine totality. Having swept away every form of so-called "higher" corporate will, he invested the individual human wills, thus left in possession of the field, with a control of their own destinies.

He fought this battle not only against the philosophy of the Absolute but against that strain in Christian theology in which the emphasis is placed on divine omnipotence. If God's will is the creative source and providential cause of all things, he must be held *responsible* for all things, including evil things; and to worship such a God must, he thought, compromise the moral will which treats evil as its enemy. If there is to be a Divine Will which is at the same time a good will, it must be one will among others, a partisan of the good, with which good men are allied — or, rather, with which they freely ally themselves in their struggle for the ideal, and in which they put their trust.

7

The human individual is for James not only a particular, a center of will, an ultimate reality in its own terms, a will possessed of freedom both from physical necessity and from wholes of which it forms a part; it is also a potent cause of historical events. Early in his career James engaged in a controversy with Grant Allen and others, who attributed historical changes exclusively to social, economic, or other over-individual causes, and conceived individual men as their passive and helpless victims. He rejected, and would today reject, every form of historicism which disparages the rôle of the individual agent; and he imputed to the "great man," and to any man who makes up his mind and pursues his ends with resolution and courage, a significant influence on the course of events — an influence which may, given a favorable conjunction of circumstances, be decisive or epoch-making.

Resuming his earlier psychological emphasis on the strain and effort of the will, James was impressed by what he called the latent "energies of men," displayed in religion, war, and discovery: reserves by which men are enabled to meet great emergencies, endure extraordinary vicissitudes, and perform prodigies of valor. Here, James thought, lie potentialities of vigorous individual living which normally remain untapped, but which could be activated, and harnessed to the pursuit of the moral ideal.

8

The willing individual, according to James, is not only the effective champion of good, but is also the stuff of which good is made. "So far as I feel anything good," he said, "I make it so. It *is* so, for me." In other words, things are good, in so far as they are liked, enjoyed, desired, or willed by individual sentient beings, such as man. There are, therefore, in this broad generic sense, innumerably many goods — "irreducibly plural." Moral evil arises from the fact that these elementary goods "form a multifarious jungle," in which they exclude or destroy one another. The moral solution of this conflict is to save as many goods as possible, to prefer the "organizable goods," and to sacrifice the non-organizable goods, or, if possible, have them represented.[8]

James's individualism is thus to be sharply distinguished from two doctrines with which it is frequently confused, namely, egoism and monadism. According to egoism, each individual is to accept *his own* will as the criterion of moral good. Moral good is equated with good-to-me. But to James selfishness and benevolence are equally individualistic. Once good is identified with individual interest, the interest of the other individual has precisely the same claim as one's own to be reckoned in the account.

According to monadism, individuals exist in isolation, both actually and ideally, whereas for James it is of the very essence of the individual that he should be one of many individuals, and that his life should be largely concerned with relations of man to man. The moral life is a life in which the interests of two or more individuals are brought into harmony.

The whole of life, embracing many wills, is morally superior to any of its parts only when it aims to include and preserve them all. This is true not only of a social whole, but of any wider whole, such as mankind at large. If the claims of an international organization are superior

[8] R. B. Perry, *Thought and Character of William James*, 1935, Vol. II, pp. 264–5.

to those of any single nation it is because its purpose is to provide for all nations, on the condition that they shall be (as we would now express it) "peace-loving" and "non-aggressive."

In order that the wills of individuals (whether persons or nations) shall be realized collectively, it is necessary that each shall assert itself and at the same time make room for others. Both of these strains were prominent in James. The first appeared in his admiration of the individual who exerts himself, endures, and overcomes obstacles, in behalf of his own demands. The second appears in that tenderness and humanity which in James invariably triumphed over self-affirmation. There was thus in James an oscillation of emphasis between the ethics of aggression, militancy, and heroism, and the ethics of conciliation, peace, and social utility. And he was deeply concerned to find a solution of this opposition — in a "moral equivalent of war," that is, in an aggressive, militant, and heroic devotion to the cause of conciliation, peace, and social utility.

9

In 1899 James published an address entitled "On a Certain Blindness in Human Beings," of which he wrote to a friend, that it "is really the perception on which my whole individualistic philosophy is based." In his published Preface he said of this address:

> It connects itself with a definite view of the world and of our moral relations to the same. . . . I mean the pluralistic or individualistic philosophy. According to that philosophy, the truth is too great for any one actual mind, even though that mind be dubbed "the Absolute," to know the whole of it. The facts and worths of life need many cognizers to take them in. There is no point of view absolutely public and universal. . . . The practical consequence of such a philos-

ophy is the well-known democratic respect for the sacredness of individuality.[9]

The "blindness" to which this address pointed, and which it sought to correct, is the failure of each human being to understand the inwardness of other lives. Each life has to itself a warmth and glow and self-justification to which other human beings, viewing it from outside, are commonly insensitive. To overcome this blindness it is necessary to possess an imaginative sympathy which projects itself to the center of the other's life, and values it in its own terms. This understanding can never be completely achieved, for that would require *living* the other life. There is always a secret residuum of insuperable privacy. So the partial blindness which remains has to be compensated by a generous allowance of credit — or a tolerance which exceeds understanding.

And similarly, for James, each nation has its unique genius, always in some measure impenetrable to outsiders, but falling within the range of their sympathy and tolerance. Each nation has its own contribution to make; the value of peace lies not merely in its prevention of destruction, but in its enabling each nation to enrich the totality of civilization through a free opportunity to be its own inimitable self.

Thus for James tolerance was not a negative or indifferent *permitting* of others to be themselves. It was attended with humility — with a positive affirmation of something that lies beyond one's power to grasp. And it was attended with a gladness that this is so, since the total value of human life lies in its inexhaustible variety, in a richness which no single mind can wholly comprehend whether by thought or by feeling.

James's mind and heart never felt overcrowded; nor was

[9] *Ibid.*, Vol. II, pp. 265–6.

he fastidious. He had an almost Whitmanesque relish for life. Some, he suggested, may shrink from the idea of immortality on the ground that the future world would be promiscuously overpopulated. But James had no interest in an exclusive Heaven of congenial spirits. "The Deity that suffers us," he said, "can suffer many another queer and wondrous and only half-delightful thing. . . . I am willing that every leaf that ever grew in this world's forests and rustled in the breeze should become immortal." [10]

His brother Henry had a less hearty appetite. It is reported that when he was traveling in America, and complained to William of the vulgar commercial travelers whom he encountered in the Pullman car, the latter wrote him promptly: "It's not the drummer's fault, Henry, it's your fault. God made the drummer, and Christ died for him."

10

And, finally, religion. James once said: "The invariable way in which religions are always treated as something tribal, collective, superpersonal and mysterious has ever been (to a rabid individualist like myself) a source of amusement and astonishment." [11] Speaking to a friend of her membership in the church, James asked her if she did not feel "shackled." When she said that, on the contrary, she felt uplifted and fortified by her sense of belonging to something greater than herself, James replied: "When *I* think of religion I imagine myself on a blasted heath, the wind blowing about my bald head, a single star above, and a profound sense of isolation." [12]

According to James the heart of religion, be it the insight of the seer or the piety of the common believer, is to

[10] *Ibid.*, Vol. II, p. 268.

[11] *Ibid.*, Vol. II, p. 347.

[12] The author owes this story to Mrs. Edward S. Drown, of Cambridge, Massachusetts.

be found in the experience and faith of the individual. The "religious experience" in the distinctive sense, is the individual's feeling of a sort of spiritual blood transfusion, that seems to come from some superhuman well-spring of energy to which he gives the name of God. He may, as in conversion, experience a radical alteration of his personality; or he may experience a reënforcement of his existing will. Because of this individualistic emphasis James was clearly in the line of the Protestant tradition; and because he stressed the specific and exceptional character of the personal religious experience, he felt, and expressed, a sympathy with evangelicism and supernaturalism.

This idea of God, James thought, derives support from the findings of psychical research and from the psychological hypothesis of a "subliminal consciousness." But it is of the essence of religion that it should pass from the sphere of science to the sphere of faith. Faiths cannot be theoretically justified — if they could they would cease to be faiths, for faith is "over-belief," that is, believing too much, as judged by strict theoretical standards.

But the act of faith has its own justification, on practical grounds. A faith which flies in the face of the facts is practically disastrous, as well as theoretically false; but a faith which is as yet not contradicted by the facts, which is factually permissible, even though not factually verifiable, may serve as a moral tonic, make life worth living, and enable the man of faith to surmount obstacles which would otherwise be impassable. Religious faith is not only faith, but it is faith in the triumph of the good. Faith in a *future* triumph of the good is not contradicted by the facts, for the faith itself may through its effect upon the will bring about the triumph, and so cause the very events by which its truth will be proved.

The triumph of the good — long-postponed, contingent on the effort, intelligence, and fidelity of the moral will —

takes place, if and when it does take place, within a reluctant universe. The evil and indifference, though they may ultimately be overcome, are not less real than the good; goodness is not a condition of existence. James's limited optimism, his "meliorism," his "fideism," are expressly opposed to all of those philosophies and religions in which men are taught a perfect trust and assurance, on the ground that all things work together for good because they derive their very being from their goodness. Some things, thought James, work against good, and many things do not care one way or the other. Individual men are themselves entrusted with the fate of the good; its fortunes depend largely on them; their responsibility is inescapable.

God, for there is still a God, is the mightiest champion of the good, whose championship is the chief ground of hope, the chief guarantee of victory. But trust in God does not mean leaving it to God. Not "God wills," but "I will, so help me God." It is God who makes possible, probable, or even seemingly certain, a success which would otherwise be incredible, so largely does it go against the grain of nature and history.

So we are brought back to the individual man, and to that strange blend of attributes which gives him what nobility he has: his sense of his own limitations and of almost insuperable resistance, coupled with fidelity to the good as he sees it, and with a willingness to risk a failure whose magnitude corresponds to the greatness of the undertaking. This is the heart of William James's philosophical attitude and the essence of that cast of mind which is characteristically American.

11

James's concrete particularism, his dynamic pluralism, his moral humanism, his practical optimism, are profoundly congenial to that Americanism, of which they are an authentic expression, and to which they have given both a philosophical sanction and a reënforcement of personal influence. James has been, and continues to be, widely read; and his influence is by no means restricted to philosophical circles. His Americanism was so central as to pervade his judgment in diverse fields of American culture.

James expressed himself profusely on questions of art and literature. Although he was himself a painter, and for some years hesitated between the vocations of art and science, he felt a profound antipathy to aestheticism; that is, to the subordination of moral to aesthetic values. He saw in aestheticism an evasion of moral responsibility, and a weakening of the moral will. To enjoy the struggle between good and evil as a spectacle is to be neutral, and to condone for the sake of its dramatic values that evil enemy which it is the business of the moral will to destroy. Hence he could speak with conviction — with American conviction — of the "rottenness," the "sweet decay" of Italy, the home of art lovers.[13]

Throughout the many years of their affectionate companionship William tried, without the slightest success, to persuade his brother Henry to write novels as he, William, would have written them. The adjectives which William applied to his brother's writings agreed essentially with the verdict of popular opinion in America: "thin," "cold," "priggish," "curly," lacking in "heartiness," "fatness," and "bigness," "too refined, too elaborate and minute." [14] Finally, in 1905, after reading *The Golden Bowl*, and reluctantly conceding its merits, William delivered himself to Henry as follows:

13 R. B. Perry, *Thought and Character of William James, Briefer Version,* 1948, pp. 218–20.
14 *Ibid.,* pp. 101, 125, 147, 176.

But why won't you, just to please Brother, sit down and write a new book, with no twilight or mustiness in the plot, with great vigor and decisiveness in the action, no fencing in the dialogue, no psychological commentaries, and absolute straightness in the style? Publish it in my name, I will acknowledge it, and give you half the proceeds. Seriously, I wish you *would,* for you *can;* and I should think it would tempt you, to embark on a "fourth manner." [15]

There can be no doubt which of the brothers was, for better or for worse, the more American. William's criticisms reflected his general judgment that "literature has no character when full of slack and wandering and superfluity. Neither does life. *Character* everywhere demands the stern and sacrificial mood as one of its factors. *The price must be paid.*" [16] James's favorite authors, all of whom conveyed this moral emphasis, were of two groups: those who, like Emerson and Carlyle, sounded the note of individual self-reliance; and those who, like Tolstoi, Wordsworth, Whitman, Hudson, and Stevenson, testified to the inner worth of the lives of others.

To James, American democracy meant the form of society which gave the individual the maximum of personal freedom; not a rigid Procrustean bed to which the individual must accommodate himself, but the unpredictable resultant of individual wills and idiosyncrasies — a whole which is the product of its own parts. Such a society would, like James's own mind, be open. It would be unafraid of the future and would look upon change as opportunity and adventure. For James could say generally what he once wrote to a friend about the emancipation of women, "I'm glad it's come. I'm glad I've lived to see it." [17]

[15] *Ibid.,* p. 335.

[16] R. B. Perry, *Thought and Character of William James,* 1935, Vol. II, p. 271.

[17] *Ibid.,* Vol. II, p. 688.

12

James was too widely traveled, both in body and in mind, to be an uncritical American nativist. He was a homesick young student of twenty-seven when he wrote the following to his family from Dresden. He had just ➤ borrowed and devoured five *Weekly Transcripts:*

> I never should have believed that in three months the tone of a Boston paper would seem so outlandish to me. As it was, I was in one squeal of amusement, surprise, and satisfaction until deep in the night when I went to bed tired out with patriotism. The boisterous animal good-humor, familiarity, reckless energy and self-confidence, unprincipled optimism, aesthetic saplessness and intellectual imbecility, made a mixture hard to characterize, but totally different from the tone of things here and, as the Germans would say, whose "Existenz so völlig dasteht" that there was nothing to do but to let yourself feel it.[18]

Fifteen years later, in 1882, he wrote again of America from Germany:

> We are a sound country and my opinion of our essential worth has risen and not fallen. We only lack abdominal depth of temperament and the power to sit for an hour over a single pot of beer without being able to tell at the end of it what we've been thinking about.[19]

In an essay entitled "The Gospel of Relaxation" James addressed himself to what he called "the hygiene of our American life," and criticized our "bottled-lightning" quality, our over-excitability and our tension, our tendency to accept as an index of energy what may be only a "habit of jerkiness and bad coördination," our "need of feeling responsible all the livelong day."[20]

[18] *Thought and Character of William James, Briefer Version,* 1948, p. 82.
[19] *Ibid.,* p. 151.
[20] James, *Essays on Faith and Morals,* 1943, pp. 238, 247, 250, 258.

These examples will suffice to show that for James Americanism was a mixture of good and bad, in which for him the good prevailed and the bad was curable. He saw the virtues of American life, and he saw its vices — in particular the vices of its virtues. He did not admire America unqualifiedly, but he admired the ideal America, which he thought to be characteristically American, as he thought it to be characteristic of America to have an ideal.

He saw that American buoyancy and self-confidence tended to a shallow optimism, that American energy tended to assume the coarser forms, and that American good-fellowship and communicativeness tended to vulgarity. But he did not believe that they needed to do so. It was his aim as a critic and reformer to make America true to her better self, and to help her to realize her higher potentialities.

When in his later years the name of James was identified with Pragmatism, he was subjected to all the misrepresentations which this school of thought invited. Construed superficially, and in terms of the language which it employed and to which it gave a wide vogue, it appeared to confirm the world's worst suspicions of Americanism. Was not America flagrantly addicted to the pursuit and worship of "success," and was Pragmatism not an open avowal of this unworthy ideal? Were not Americans excessively "practical," and did not Pragmatism proclaim the supremacy of the practical over the theoretical and the aesthetic, and even call itself by the name of "practicalism"? Was it not a notorious fact that Americans were commercially-minded, and did not James speak of truth in terms of the "cash-value" of ideas? Was it not an American fault to measure attainment in quantitative terms, to evade the profundities of metaphysics, to substitute short for long-range goals and expediency for principle, and did not James confirm and glorify these faults? Was America not deplorably lacking in saints and sages, and did not James write in the vernacular and echo the popular vulgarisms?

The only corrective of these charges is to read James in context and to make the acquaintance of the man himself. He resented the description of Pragmatism "as a characteristically American movement, a sort of bobtailed scheme of thought, excellently fitted for the man on the street, who naturally hates theory and wants cash returns immediately." [21] As he repeatedly pointed out, neither he nor his associates had ever intended to interpret "practical" in any narrow or debasing sense. He did not consider it a disparagement of theory to construe knowledge in terms of a pursuit of truth, or to affirm that truth was useful, or to insist that the meaning and truth of ideas lie in the particular consequences of practice and experience to which they lead. His empiricism did not imply any rejection of metaphysics; on the contrary, he hoped that it might rid metaphysics of the occult and the dogmatic, and establish it on a sound basis comparable to that of science.

It was James himself who labeled "Success" the "bitch-goddess," having in mind easy or merely material success.[22] He was profoundly concerned with the *kind* of success on which men set their hearts. For after all, is not the salvation of the soul a kind of success? Does not the devotee of pure science, or the creative artist, or the exponent of higher culture, or the social reformer, hope for success? For merely quantitative success, mere bigness of achievement, measured in terms of population, money, territory, or popular acclaim, James had the utmost contempt. He admired American energy, but he admired its finer, and deprecated its grosser, forms. As for "cash-value," it ought

[21] *Meaning of Truth,* 1909, p. 185.

[22] In a letter to H. G. Wells, *Letters of William James,* 1920, Vol. II, p. 260.

not to be necessary to say that he did not refer to money, but to first-hand experience, on whatever level, and including the level of religious mysticism.

James was not the enemy of meditation, gentleness, and the finer arts: of all places in the world James would have felt most out of place in the market-place. He was the enemy of authority and dogma, of fatalism, despair, and escapism, of stagnation, of inhumanity, and of the oppressive weight of established things. He was the friend of collective hope in a changing world — of hope based on the resolution and concerted efforts of responsible individuals. And in this friendship he believed that he was at the same time the loyal friend of his America. For though he frequently and emphatically condemned America, he believed that he judged America by American standards.

IV

The American
Religious Heritage

1

RELIGION IS AN ATTITUDE of belief, rather than a theoretic or discursive process, and tends by most people, most of the time, to be taken for granted. When it is said, as can be truly said, that America is a "Christian country," or is a part of "Christendom," this does not mean that all Americans, or even many Americans, spend their time formulating and arguing a body of theological doctrine, but that they proceed on certain assumptions, which they invoke at moments of crisis, which they defend against attack, to which they say "yes," or "I suppose so," when they are asked, and which are explicitly defined only by those among their members who do their thinking for them.

It is inaccurate to say that America is a "Christian" country if the term Christian be taken to exclude Judaism. It is one of the most fantastic effects of human bigotry that so many Christians forget that Jesus was a Jew, and that the greater part of the Bible which they read is a record of Jewish history and an expression of Jewish culture and institutions. Except for the accidents of race and persecution, Judaism might have been regarded as a branch of Christianity, or Christianity as a branch of Judaism, differing on points scarcely more fundamental than those which divide one sect of Christianity or of Judaism from another.

When Catholics, Protestants, and Jews sit amicably together on a platform, they are bound by much more than their common cult of tolerance. They are bound by a Hebraic-Christian tradition which is characteristically American, which is transmitted from generation to generation by the teachings of childhood, which is continuously affirmed by American churches of all descriptions, and which is nourished by the universal reading and re-reading of the English Bible, Old and New Testaments alike, as well as of that great body of literature through which Biblical words, metaphors, and forms of thought have been widely diffused.[1]

The general Hebraic-Christian-Biblical tradition embraces ideas so familiar that, like the air, they are inhaled without effort or attention. The most fundamental of these is the idea of one personal God, the Creator of nature and the ruler of mankind, flanking human life on all sides — above, below, at the beginning, and at the end, of time. This God is invested with the parental attributes: like a father he both loves and chastens his human children; who, having erred, are restored to favor and perfected in their innate attributes by a way of salvation exemplified, if not mediated, by Jesus of Nazareth. Within this broad framework there is room for countless differences of detail in matters of dogma and worship, for differences of pious fervor, and for differences of strictness.

Where, as in America, this theistic belief is traditional and pervasive, it determines disbelief as well as belief. It

[1] Jews, as such, have of course played an important rôle in American development, but not comparable in importance to that played by Hebraic ideas embraced under the name of Christianity. Whenever, as, for example, in Puritanism, emphasis has been on the Old Testament, it is proper to credit the special influence of Judaism. Cf. Oscar S. Strauss, *The Origin of Republican Form of Government in the U. S. of America*, 1926; and Elisha M. Friedman, *Israel of Tomorrow*, Herald Square Press, Inc., N. Y., 1946, pp. 411–14.

is the rejection of this belief that characterizes American atheism; it is the dilution of this belief that constitutes American liberal religion; and it is the half-heartedness of this belief that constitutes American irreligion. It has been said of the liberalized requirement for the presidency of a certain sectarian college that "a Baptist is a man who, when he stays away from church, stays away from the Baptist church." Theism in the broad Hebraic-Christian-Biblical sense is in America the norm both of fidelity and of infidelity.

The personal and social implications of this broad creed are apparent. It raises mankind to the dignity of possessing a family likeness to the maker of the universe. It makes of each human being an object of compassion and solicitude, such as the parent feels for the child regardless of his talents or merit; so that it is love rather than strict justice that speaks the last word. It thus enlivens the pacifist and humanitarian sentiments, and supports social legislation designed to mitigate cruelty and misery. It encourages in each erring individual human being a sense of ingratitude and unworthiness, and at the same time a sense of high destiny and hopefulness; and thus supports the idea of progress. It unites human beings through the sense of their equality before God and their fraternity as his children; and thus supports the idea of internationalism. It gives to the moral or spiritual life of man a cosmic validity, which raises it above man-made institutions, such as the state or the civil law.

The Hebraic-Christian belief thus constitutes a persistent focus of resistance to political tyranny based on the lower sanctions of power or legitimacy. Both Christianity and Judaism have in the past been persecuted minorities prepared to suffer at the hands of temporal authorities for the sake of principle. The moral and spiritual life of man constitutes the central plot of the drama of history — with all its struggles and vicissitudes, and with its happy ending whether in this world or the next. Duty and aspiration are reënforced through being identified with the will of a God who both commands and entreats.

Hebraic-Christian theism in this generalized sense is American, both really, and nominally or officially. Its reality lies in its tacit assumption as a basis for American practice. It is intimately allied with that benevolent individualism, that sense of a moral and spiritual mission, and that practical and persevering optimism, which characterizes the temper of the American mind. Nominally and officially it appears in the formal recognition of theism through the appointment of chaplains to Congress and the armed services, the motto "In God We Trust" stamped on silver coins, and the profession of belief in God by political leaders, from Deists and Unitarians on the left to Roman Catholics on the right.

2

The Protestant tendency to a multiplication of sects has had free play in America. This has forced a separation of Church and State and a policy of religious tolerance, which, in turn, have promoted the sectarianism which was their principal cause.

Sectarianism in America began early, reflecting conditions in the mother country, and it has continued unabated. It was in 1647 that Nathaniel Ward voiced the following complaint, in his *Simple Cobler of Aggawam in America:*

> I lived in a City, where a Papist Preached in one Church, a Lutheran in another, a Calvinist in a third; a Lutheran one part of the day, a Calvinist the other, in the same Pulpit: the Religion of that place was but motl[e]y and meagre, their affections Leopard-like.[2]

[2] *Simple Cobler of Aggawam in America,* 1647, p. 5.

Ward was an exponent of New England theocracy who deprecated the motley and leopard-like complexion of religion in the Seventeenth Century. He spoke for the losing cause of intolerant uniformity. The following description of Missouri in 1820 was written from the reverse point of view of one who deprecated the narrow bigotry of worshippers that "split on trifling differences"; but the picture resembles that of New England drawn by Ward nearly two centuries before:

> At one point you meet with a respectable Methodist, and begin to feel an attachment to the profession . . . and the next thing which you hear, is, that you are charged with being a fierce Calvinist, and that you have preached that "hell is paved with infants' skulls." While, perhaps the society, with which you are connected, hear from an opposite quarter . . . that in such a sermon you departed from the dicta of the great master, and are leading the people to the gulph of Arminianism. The Baptists are as exclusive as in the older regions. Even among our own brethren, it is well known, that there is some feeling of a questionable nature, some rivalry between the pupils, the doctors, and schools, of Andover and Princeton. The Cumberland Presbyterians, with all the freshness of a new sect, are not found lacking in this order of things. Lastly, there are the Catholics, abundantly more united in faith, in spirit, and in purpose, than we are, — who claim a kind of prescriptive right to the ground, on the pretext of prior possession. . . . Add to these the followers of Elias Smith, and multitudes of men who would be founders of new sects, and who erect their own standard in the wilderness, and you will have some idea of the sectarian feelings that you will have to encounter.[3]

Sects originating in America have been American not only in their multiplicity but in their specific characteristics. Mormonism was a sort of Americanism in miniature: in its republicanism, its emphasis on compact in both church and polity, its association of piety with conquest

[3] Timothy Flint, *Recollections of the Last Ten Years*, 1826 [reprinted, 1932], pp. 110, 111–12. Flint was a Presbyterian missionary.

and adventure, its sense of destiny, its resourcefulness and capacity for organization. Christian Science is profoundly different, but not less American: in its practical emphasis, its optimism, its identification of religion with health, and its reconciliation of religion with the possession and enjoyment of this world's goods.

Multi-sectarianism springs from that very aspect of Protestantism which is most profoundly in agreement with the American temper of mind. The Protestant is encouraged to make up his own mind, and to speak and act on it. If he has an idea which he thinks important he campaigns for it; and, having won adherents, he organizes them with the intent of saving the balance of mankind. These are things which might equally well be said of Americans in general.

3

Calvinism is not a peculiarity of colonial New England, but a part of the heroic legend of America. There are two explanations of the English settlements on the Atlantic sea-coast in the early decades of the Seventeenth Century. According to one theory, the immigrants were impelled by religious motives; according to the second, their motives were economic and political, expressing the expansionist and adventuring spirit of the Elizabethan era. But if the colonists were governed by mixed motives, seeing in the new settlements a double opportunity — of serving God *and* of finding opportunity of employment and wealth — they were no more than human.

The tendency to emphasize the rôle of the New Englanders and to belittle that of the Virginians, even at the expense of historical accuracy, is itself a manifestation of the American mind as this came over the years to find itself and to create its own myths. The difference, broadly speaking, between these two areas of settlement — between John

Smith and John Winthrop or William Bradford — lay in the comparatively greater extent to which the New England settlers, both the Pilgrims of Plymouth and the Puritans proper of Massachusetts Bay, felt themselves to be dedicated collectively to a holy mission.

In the course of the last 300 years America has grown from a handful of exiles on the edge of a wilderness to the mightiest of world powers. But there is an identity and thread of continuity which spans this interval of growth. When John Cotton bade godspeed to the Winthrop party in 1630, he exhorted them to look well to their "plantation," and cultivate "public spirit," "universal helpfulness," care of their children, and kindness to the "poor natives," whom they were to feed with "spirituals" in exchange for their "temporals." He assured them that if their planting was God's planting it would not be rooted up but would "prosper and flourish." [4] The plantation which Cotton had in mind was not a tobacco plantation, but a moral plantation bearing fruits of righteousness. When Americans today feel a peculiar responsibility for the planting of a peace based on justice and humanity, they are expressing in new ways and under new conditions the genius of this ancestral soul.

The anti-Calvinistic protest is not to be underestimated — it constitutes a persistent and central theme in the American religious consciousness. But it is to be noted that Calvinism itself provided many of the weapons with which it was attacked. William Ellery Channing, the great exponent of American Unitarianism, is a case in point. Unitarianism itself arose in New England, as a dissident branch of Congregational Puritanism. Channing's anti-Calvinistic argument was directed against the "immoral" conception of a deity who condemned mankind to helpless depravity

---

[4] *God's Promise to His Plantation*, 1630 (reprinted in *Old South Leaflets*, Vol. III, No. 53) , pp. 13–15.

and then saved a minority from perpetual torture by the exercise of an arbitrary clemency. And when Calvinists supported their sombre view by pleading human ignorance of God's inscrutable ways, Channing could appeal to Calvinism itself as having taught men to rely on their own conscience and judgment.[5]

Calvinism, in short, was woven of two conflicting strands: the prostration of man before an autocratic God, and the exaltation of man as a responsible and autonomous being. This same inner conflict appeared in the field of church polity: its theocratic authoritarianism, and its congregational democracy. The same stubborn self-reliance with which Calvinists defied the temporal authorities led them in the long run to defy their own ecclesiastical authorities. Calvinism was pessimistic in its emphasis on human sin and inability; but it also contained the seeds of optimism, since it taught men to think for themselves and to believe in the power, both long-range and short-range, of the disciplined moral will. It was this "good" Calvinism which was absorbed into the main stream of American thought and sentiment — though it is the bad Calvinism which has usually appropriated the name.

The influence of Calvinism, good and bad, is not to be restricted to New England Puritanism of the colonial period. As for the Anglicans, it must be remembered that Virginia was settled in 1607, when Puritans were still a reforming group within the established church of England; and there were many such among the Virginia settlers. Furthermore, owing to absence of episcopal control, the Anglican churches of Virginia were governed by vestries, which, like the consistories, sessions, and boards of deacons and elders in non-Anglican churches, set a pattern for representative civil government. The great Virginians of

[5] Cf. "The Moral Argument Against Calvinism," *Works*, Vol. I (1841), pp. 217–41.

the colonial and revolutionary days thus found in the Anglican church a school of republicanism similar to that of the non-Anglican Calvinistic churches.[6]

Nor should the Virginia settlement be identified with the Cavalier anti-Puritanism which developed in Britain at the time of the Puritan Revolution and the Restoration. It is true that they were not bound together, as were the settlers of Plymouth and Massachusetts Bay, by reforming zeal. But they were regarded in New England not as anti-Puritans, but rather as Puritans who "have . . . lost even the sap of grace, and edge to all goodness, and are become mere worldlings." [7]

Calvinism of various types may be said to have dominated American Protestant Christianity during the Seventeenth Century, and it was powerfully reënforced in the century that followed. The highly prolific New England Puritans who migrated to the West took their Puritanism with them. Presbyterian Calvinism entered America with the Scotch and the Scotch-Irish, and was transmitted to their numerous and widely scattered descendants. Continental Protestantism of the Reformed or Calvinistic variety entered America with the French Huguenots, with the Dutch, and with the Germans and Swiss. But Calvinism owed its paramount influence not only to the number of its professed adherents and their wide distribution, but to their zeal, and to the industry and thrift which were sanctioned by their piety.

4

Evangelism in the broad sense is inherent in the genius of Christianity, and missionaries have played an important

[6] Cf. Benjamin Rice Lacy, Jr., "A Dynamic Tradition," in *Our Protestant Heritage,* John Knox Press, Richmond, Virginia, 1948.

[7] Robert Cushman, "Discourse" of Dec. 9, 1621, *Chronicles of the Pilgrim Fathers* (Everyman's Library), p. 235; cf. the Author's *Puritanism and Democracy,* 1944, pp. 78–81.

rôle in the extension of American territory and influence, beginning with the Christianizing of the hapless American Indians by Puritans, Jesuits, and Benedictines, and afterwards continued by all Christian-American sects both at home and abroad. The home missions on the advancing western frontier were concerned not so much with spreading the gospel as with bringing support to its scattered outposts. It is owing largely to this form of evangelism that sectarian colleges have been dispersed throughout the country, which, once established, have gradually departed in greater or lesser degree from their original sectarian dogmas. This religious impulse has been the greatest single force in the development of American higher education, gradually outweighed, but never superseded, by the development of the secular universities, private and public.

The periodic "revival," due to the tendency of piety to lapse into indifference and external observance, is a universal religious phenomenon. But in a narrower and more specific sense the term "evangelical" refers to two great sects, the Methodist and the Baptist; whose growth was stimulated by the "Great Awakening" and the preaching of John Wesley and George Whitefield in the Eighteenth Century, and accelerated by numerous revivalists and evangelists during the century that followed.

The Methodists and Baptists now constitute the two largest Protestant groups. Their ministry and churches vary greatly in different sections of the country, reflecting local conditions. Both sects have contributed leaders of thought, and of educational and social progress. But it is not an accident that they spread most rapidly in the West and South on the edge of the advancing frontier. This can be explained by the comparative simplicity of their appeal. Their preachers, during the period of their most rapid advance, possessed a rude eloquence which suited the temper of the unsophisticated. Although they were individualistic in their emphasis, they profited, through the "camp-meeting," by the emotional contagion of the crowd. Rejecting or abandoning the Calvinistic dogma of the "elect," they promised salvation to all repentant sinners. Their spirit was, and remains, equalitarian, humanitarian, and utopian. Owing largely to the spread of these evangelical sects in America, the church has never become, as in Europe, an "estate," aligned with a military caste, or economic aristocracy, or intellectual élite, in defense of existing privilege and authority.[8]

5

From the standpoint of foreign observers the most striking feature of religion in America is the absence of any sharp alignment of irreligion against religion, or of anticlericalism against clericalism, such as exists throughout the greater part of Christendom. A primary cause of this phenomenon is the middle ground afforded by the vogue of Deism among the leaders of thought in the Revolutionary period: Jefferson and Franklin were "mild Deists"; and even Thomas Paine was not lacking in religious piety. Although the epithet of "atheism" is often applied to all theism that falls short of some standard of orthodoxy, Deism was, as the name clearly implies, a form of theism. Its essence lay not in its denial of God, but in its affirmation of God on strictly rational grounds. God was argued from nature as its first and intelligent cause, and from conscience as the sanction of duty. Like mathematics and natural science this body of argument was considered as requiring no support beyond that of man's free and natural intellectual faculties; and as such it was taught to successive generations of American youth.

The older Deism, which was in good repute in America

[8] Cf. W. W. Sweet, *Revivalism in America,* 1944.

in the Age of the Enlightenment, was continued in later years under the broader name of "liberal religion." American Protestantism has always been vulnerable in America to Biblical criticism, to the teachings of science, and to the methods of scientific inquiry.

Thus from the Atheism of Robert Ingersoll on the extreme left, through Unitarian Humanism and the liberal parties in each of the Protestant sects, to fundamentalism and rigid orthodoxy on the right, every shade of opinion, or degree of fervor, or of strictness, has come to be represented. There is a continuity of more or less, all along the line. Similarly it is not possible in America to draw a sharp line between religion and various secular groups designed for self-improvement or social reform. It is impossible to understand America without taking account of the large amount of piety which finds expression outside of the church.

Within the Protestant churches themselves the secular impulse tends to shift the emphasis from theological doctrine to ethics. When religious orthodoxy declines, the effect in America is not to develop an anti-clericalism or skepticism, but a "practical Christianity," which concentrates attention on the humanitarian teaching and example of Jesus. This "Social Gospel Movement," as it came to be called toward the end of the Nineteenth Century, was represented by one of the best-selling best sellers of all time, Charles M. Sheldon's *In His Steps,* of which 8,000,000 copies are said to have been sold in the United States. With Walter Rauschenbusch,[9] Washington Gladden, Shailer Mathews and others, at the opening of the present century, the movement addressed itself to the causes of social evil — to political corruption, and the economic condition of the

[9] The titles of Rauschenbusch's works are significant: *Christianity and the Social Crisis,* 1907; *Prayers of the Social Awakening,* 1910; *Christianizing the Social Order,* 1912.

unprivileged classes — and was taken over as the social creed of the Protestant churches.

Owing to this strong social emphasis, Christianity in America has not been invoked merely to reconcile man to the *status quo* — to substitute "pie in the sky" for the immediate and tangible benefits of economic reform. Hence religion has not been considered as the enemy of the labor movement, and other forms of the "social revolution." This is one of the reasons why orthodox Marxism has gained so slight a foothold in America. On the whole, American Christianity has not been an "opiate," but rather a stimulant and eye-opener, of the poor.

6

While American Protestantism has tended to sectarianism and to various shadings of liberalism and secularism, the focus of religious orthodoxy and pious fervor has shifted toward Catholicism. The Catholic population rose rapidly during the last century, owing to the large immigrations from Ireland, Germany, Canada, Italy and Poland. According to recent published statistics, of the 77,386,188 people professing allegiance to a religious group, 46,149,676 are members of Protestant denominations; while 25,286,178 are reported as members of the Roman Catholic Church. The Catholic rate of increase exceeds that of the whole body of Protestants.[10] These figures do not, however, adequately represent the actual situation, for Catholicism is one church united at home and abroad, and relatively uniform in discipline, doctrine, and worship; while Protestantism, on the other hand, has only a nominal unity, or a loose, voluntary, and occasional federation. The largest groups, the Baptists with 12½ millions, and the Methodists with 8½ millions, are themselves

<hr>

[10] *New York Times,* July 26, 1948, p. 19.

split into several opposing factions. It is fair to say, therefore, that Catholicism is much the most powerful single organized religious force in the United States, and that this preponderance is likely to increase in the future.

Over and above its strength as an organized church, Catholicism enjoys many advantages: its antiquity; its pageantry and color; its varied and graded assortment of ideas, enabling it to offer ready answers to all questions, whether from the learned or the ignorant; its intimate concern with birth, death, marriage and other crucial and universal phases of human life; its inclusion of the supernatural and miraculous; its consolation of the afflicted; its elaborate and continuous program of pious observance, with confession, penitence, prayer, and calendar of saints days; and its clearly marked identity, through resistance to compromise and the encroachments of secularism.

Until recently Catholicism has been on the defensive in America. Despite the small Catholic enclave in Maryland, Catholics were in colonial days a suspected minority, persecuted, or at best reluctantly tolerated. During the Nineteenth Century America was repeatedly swept by waves of anti-Catholic hostility — often breaking into violence and bloodshed. This was in fact only one chapter of the history of intolerance and mob action, of which non-Catholic sects and non-religious groups were also frequently the victims. But the anti-Catholic sentiment was peculiarly persistent and widespread, culminating in the "Know Nothing" movement which under various labels and slogans achieved considerable political power in the 1850's, and in the Ku Klux Klan seventy years later.[11]

The reasons for this anti-Catholicism are evident and familiar. The colonies of the eastern seaboard were settled in the main by Protestants when "Romishness" and

[11] For a full description of anti-Catholic persecution in America, cf. Mauritz Hallgren, *Landscape of Freedom*, 1941.

"Popery" were the objects of implacable enmity. Their migration was, in fact, a chapter in the history of the Protestant Reformation. The struggle among the great European colonial powers for control of the New World coincided with the struggle between Catholicism and Protestantism, and the victory of England over Spain and France was a victory of Protestantism. Catholic ultramontanism was opposed by American nativism and nationalism; Catholic ritualism and sacramentalism were opposed in the name of simplicity of worship; Catholic dogmatism was opposed by rationalism; Catholic ecclesiasticism, associated with authoritarianism and the institution of monarchy, was opposed by republicanism; the Catholic discipline and solidarity, especially as represented by the Jesuit Order, were suspected of secret conspiracy. To these grounds of hostility were added differences of race and social status. The low standard of living of Catholic immigrants appeared to be a threat to American labor. Settling en masse in the larger American cities, they tended to the lower economic and social levels, separated by a wide gulf from American leadership in the arts and professions, as well as in finance, commerce, and industry.

This anti-Catholic hostility was not exclusively an effect of ignorance and mob-psychology. It was as marked in the contempt of the intelligentsia as in the violence of the masses. Emerson wrote of his attitude toward his young friend, Isaac Hecker, who had been converted to Catholicism:

> Nor could I possibly affect the smallest interest in anything that regarded his church. We are used to this whim of a man's choosing to put on and wear a painted petticoat, as we are to whims of artists who wear a mediaeval cap or beard, . . . but, of course, they must say nothing about it to us, and we will never notice it to them, but will carry on general conversation, with utter reticence as to each other's whimsies; but if once they speak of it, they are not

107

the men we took them for, and we do not talk with them twice.[12]

The overwhelming defeat of Al Smith in 1930, despite his great ability and popularity, proved the persistence of anti-Catholic sentiment, especially in rural communities; but his repeated election to the Governorship of New York, and his nomination for the Presidency, were evidence of the strengthened position of Catholicism. Respect for the opinion of Catholic voters influences to an increasing extent both domestic legislation and foreign policy.

It is timely to ask, therefore, how far Catholicism is or is not in fundamental agreement with the American national creed. This is a subject which must not be left either to apologists or to detractors. Nor is it wise to reach hasty conclusions on a matter of such gravity.[13]

7

To those who hope for a reconciliation of Catholicism and Americanism the history of the Nineteenth Century is by no means reassuring. It is scarcely too much to say that this century witnessed a second Counter-Reformation, in which the object of Catholic attack was not Protestantism or any other dissenting church or religious sect, but the modern spirit in general, as this manifested itself in diverse fields of human activity, political, social, scientific and cultural.

But this oversimplified statement obscures the heart of the matter. It will not do to trust the catchwords used either by the critics of Catholicism or by its proponents. It is true that Catholicism has avowedly rejected what it

[12] Entry made in the year 1862, *Journals of Ralph Waldo Emerson,* edited by E. W. Emerson and W. E. Forbes, 1913, Vol. IX, pp. 467-8.

[13] Certain portions of this topic have been more fully treated in the Author's "Catholicism and Modern Liberalism," *Proceedings of the American Catholic Philosophical Association,* 1943.

calls "democracy," "liberalism," "modernism," and even "Americanism." But it has, nevertheless, been domesticated in America; it has lived on in the modern age; its teachings have reflected the liberal tendencies of its place and time; and its adherents have been at one and the same time good Catholics and good democrats. The key to this seeming paradox lies in the fact that Catholicism is divisible into two parts: its social doctrine, and its claim to authority.

It is in the encyclicals of Leo XIII that the concessions of Catholicism to the modern age are most apparent. It was apparent to this astute statesman that if Catholicism was to compete with the secular state it must promise equivalent or greater advantages in terms of welfare, progress, and democratic government. In his encyclical letter of November 1, 1885, *Immortale Dei,* or "The Christian Constitution of States," Leo XIII argued that, although the Church was founded to save souls, "yet in regard to things temporal she is the source of benefits as manifold and as great as if the chief end of her existence were to ensure the prospering of our earthly life." The Church, he said, welcomed every advance of knowledge and of the industrial arts: "Our eyes are not closed to the spirit of the times. We do not repudiate the assured and useful improvements of our age. The Church does not condemn either monarchy or republic, or any greater or less share of the people in the exercise of political power." [14]

In the *Rerum Novarum,* published in 1891, and sometimes entitled "The Condition of the Working Classes," this same Pope turned his attention to the social evils growing out of the Industrial Revolution. His position was advanced and bold. He condemned the exploitation of the poor by the rich, even when this takes the form of

[14] Quoted in Philip Hughes, *The Pope's New Order,* 1944, pp. 89, 99, 100.

voluntary contract. While defending private property against socialism, he insisted on the public duties which accompanied its possession. He advocated trade unions and collective bargaining, and the intervention of the state to insure proper wages and conditions and hours of labor. He appealed to the whole Church to participate actively in constructive measures of social reform.

This encyclical marked the beginning of Catholic action in the economic and social field and of the creation of Catholic parties in Italy and France, which came to bear the names of "Catholic socialism" and "Catholic democracy." [15] It provided the inspiration of non-political social agencies such as the National Catholic Welfare Council in the United States. Its teachings were reaffirmed and extended by Pope Pius XI in an encyclical entitled *Forty Years After*.[16]

Catholicism was peculiarly qualified, by its insistence upon the universality of its principles, and by its own existence as a supra-national institution, to assume a position of leadership in the cause of peace. This in fact it has done. Beginning in the last century, and increasingly since the beginning of World War I, the Roman pontiffs have been largely preoccupied with this question. They have deplored war, and exposed its immoral causes and its demoralizing effects; they have refused to accept its necessity. They have denounced statism, rebuked the excesses of nationalism, and opposed the increase of armaments. They have repeatedly attempted to effect peaceful settlements. They have advocated international organization for peace and supported the League of Nations and the United Nations. Especially notable have been the efforts of Pius XI and Pius XII, who have addressed themselves to "the

[15] In his encyclical of January 18, 1901, entitled *Graves de Communi*, Leo XIII discussed the difficulty of finding a proper title for such parties: since "socialism" and "democracy" carried too radical meanings.

[16] Cf. *Forty Years After*, National Catholic Welfare Conference, 1940.

Whole World" and have refused to despair of a "new order," which should respect the rights of small states and national minorities, provide the access of all peoples to the earth's natural resources, limit armaments, and observe and extend international law.[17]

8

But at the same time that Catholic social and political philosophy marched with the times, whether in the rear or in the van, and voiced the common aspiration toward the spread of enlightenment, the increase of freedom, and the improvement of the temporal lot of mankind, Catholicism was increasingly insistent on the authority and exclusive claims of its own Church. Consistently and unremittingly, successive Popes have affirmed the priority of the religious over the secular, of Catholic Christianity over other religions, and of the Pope over the Catholic clergy and laity.

Pius IX, in his famous "Syllabus of Errors," condemned not only naturalism and rationalism in their extreme forms but "moderate rationalism," "indifferentism" and "latitudinarianism." He rejected liberty of faith, conscience, and worship, and claimed the right of the Church to control science, culture, and education. On his own authority he proclaimed the dogma of the Immaculate Conception of the Virgin Mary, and in 1870 he succeeded in obtaining acceptance of the dogma of papal infallibility.

Leo XIII's program of social reform was accompanied by the declaration that *only* the Church can save the world, promote civilization, and bring about progress. The social evils to be corrected were attributed to impatience with

17 Cf. Pius XII's radio message, "Nell'Alba," December 24, 1941, *A Papal Peace Mosaic*, 1944, published by the Catholic Association for International Peace.

authority, and in particular with the authority of the Church. This same Pope recommended the revival of the philosophy of Thomas Aquinas. This recommendation was followed up by the encyclicals of Pius X, which regulated the studies of seminarists and young clerics, with the result that philosophy, like matters of faith and dogma, was brought under papal direction. It was this same Pope who rooted out Catholic Modernism or drove it underground. Both this pontiff and his successor Benedict XV prescribed the duty of clerics to obey the Pope in matters social and political as well as religious.[18]

9

During the second half of the Nineteenth Century certain distinguished American Catholics sought to bring their Catholic piety into closer accord with their Americanism. Isaac Hecker, the founder of the Paulist Order, was, like Orestes Brownson, a Transcendentalist before becoming a Catholic. Like Brownson, he hoped to convert Americans to Catholicism by appealing to their better Americanism, and by showing that Catholicism was more American than was Protestantism. Except in his evangelical zeal, he might be said to have been an Emersonian, as Brownson was a Jacksonian, Catholic. His appeal was to the individual acting under the direct inspiration of God. Through this gospel of inspired self-reliance he hoped to identify Catholicism with the principles of the Declaration of Independence; with the energy and manly qualities which he so much admired in Americans; and with the spirit of the modern age:

> Men will be called for who have that universal synthesis of truth which will solve the problems, eliminate the antagonisms, and meet the great needs of the age; men who will

[18] Cf. George F. La Piana, "From Leo XIII to Benedict XV," *American Journal of Theology*, Vol. XXI (1917), pp. 183, 187.

defend and uphold the Church against the attacks which threaten her destruction, with weapons suitable to the times; men who will turn all the genuine aspirations of the age, — in science, in socialism, in politics, in spiritism, in religion, — which are now perverted against the Church, into means of her defence and universal triumph.[19]

After Father Hecker's death, certain Catholic clerics hoped for a more tolerant and flexible attitude on the part of the Church. The most notable of these was Cardinal Gibbons, of whom it has been said that he was "the champion of the Catholic Church in America and the champion of America in the Catholic Church." [20] Father Walter Elliott's *Life of Father Hecker* excited great interest among French liberals, and gave rise to a controversy that was carried to Rome. In January, 1899, Leo XIII condemned Hecker's ideas, as interpreted by his partisans, in a letter to Cardinal Gibbons "Concerning New Opinion."

From the standpoint of the Pope, "Americanism" meant dangerous thoughts — dangerous in their content, but above all in their source, since they arose at the periphery rather than at the center of the ecclesiastical system. The rebuke to Cardinal Gibbons was kindly, but firm. The Pope first quoted the decree of the Vatican Council:

> For the doctrine of faith which God has revealed has not been proposed, like a philosophical invention to be perfected by human ingenuity, but has been delivered as a divine deposit to the Spouse of Christ, to be faithfully kept and infallibly declared. Hence that meaning of the sacred dogmas is perpetually to be retained which Our Holy Mother, the Church, has once declared; nor is that meaning ever to be departed from under the pretence or pretext of a deeper comprehension of them.[21]

[19] Quoted in Henry Dwight Sedgwick, Jr., *Father Hecker*, 1900, pp. 106–8, 131–2.

[20] A. S. Will, *Life of Cardinal Gibbons*, 1922, Vol. I, p. 497.

[21] *Constitutio dogmatica de fide Catholica*, April 23, 1870, Ch. IV; quoted in H. D. Sedgwick, Jr., *op. cit.*, pp. 146–7.

He then proceeded as follows:

> But, beloved son, in this present matter of which We are speaking there is even a greater danger and a more manifest opposition to Catholic doctrine and discipline in that opinion of the lovers of novelty, according to which they hold such liberty should be allowed in the Church, that her supervision and watchfulness being in some sense lessened, allowance be granted the faithful, each one to follow out more freely the leading of his own mind and the trend of his own proper activity. They are of opinion that such liberty has its counterpart in the newly given civil freedom which is now the right and the foundation of almost every secular state. . . .
>
> We are not able to give approval to those views which, in their collective sense, are called by some "Americanism." [22]

Cardinal Gibbons's submission is thus recorded in his journal:

> March 17 1899. I sent the Holy Father a reply to his letter received February 17th on the subject of Americanism. After thanking his Holiness for dispelling the cloud of misunderstanding, I assured him that the false conceptions of Americanism emanating from Europe have no existence among the prelates, priests and Catholic laity of our country. [23]

No one has set forth the logic of the Catholic position more clearly than John L. Spalding, an American Bishop of the last century, who was in high favor with President Theodore Roosevelt:

[22] Quoted in H. D. Sedgwick, Jr., *op. cit.,* pp. 147–8, 151. For other extracts from the Pope's letter, cf. A. S. Will, *op. cit.,* pp. 553–7. The "Americanism" which Leo XIII condemned is not to be confused with another "Americanism" which was opposed to the "Cahensly movement," which had sought to preserve and promote in each immigrant group its cultural and religious ties with the mother country. Here also, Cardinal Gibbons was a good American; but here the Pope sided with him in favor of the development of an American Catholic Church which would share the language and culture of Americans.

[23] Quoted by A. S. Will, *op. cit.,* Vol. I, pp. 557–8.

The Church . . . is one in its principle of life, from which it also derives its unity of organization, of government, of doctrine, and of worship. Opposed to unity are heresy and schism. . . . Since unity is a distinctive mark of the Church, it follows at once that the whole Catholic system must necessarily rest upon the principle of authority. It is idle to talk of unity in religion where there is no supreme and infallible voice to command obedience. This infallible voice is that of the living Church.[24]

Thus the history of Catholicism during the one hundred seventy years of the national existence of the United States reveals two broad trends: a trend coinciding broadly with contemporary political, social, and economic progress; and a trend toward more rigid and highly centralized ecclesiastical authority. And whenever these two trends have come into conflict, it is the second which appears to have prevailed in Rome, while it is the first which has prevailed in America.

10

Are Catholicism and American liberalism forever irreconcilable? Is "liberal Catholicism" a contradiction in terms? Is there a common liberal ground — a secular liberalism — on which Catholic liberalism can unite with Protestant liberalism and with Americans of every shade of religious belief and unbelief?

America was conceived and born at a time when moral and political principles were largely divorced in men's minds from the tenets of any particular religious sect. The name of God appeared in the Declaration of Independence, but as a gesture of piety rather than as a premise of the argument. And to Americans ever since, the American national creed has seemed not less self-evident in itself than any religious creed from which it might be derived. The

[24] "The Catholic Church," in *Lectures and Discourses,* 1882; quoted in H. R. Warfel (ed.) , *The American Mind,* 1937, Vol. II, p. 1074.

foundations of society were laid in human nature and were immediately intelligible to the human reason. It was remarked that they were known to the pagan world before the advent of Christianity, and to Chinese and other strange peoples beyond the limits of Christendom. If ,they were authorized or commanded by God it was because they conduced to the happiness of His creatures, which any one could see by observing their operation.

This is one of the things, then, that is meant by liberalism, in its application to America — that social institutions are contrived by man for the sake of the benefits which accrue to their members, independently of any theistic or other metaphysical framework such as might be affirmed either by Protestants or Catholics, either by theists or atheists. It is this independence which has enabled it to serve as a common ground on which all Americans take their stand together.

In considering the relation of liberalism, so conceived, to Catholic Christianity, it is essential that it should be divorced from associations by which it is condemned in advance, as when it is identified with anarchism, atheism, materialism, or "individualism." Among the question-begging epithets which are applied to liberalism by its Catholic opponents, the least justified is "individualism," where the term is used to mean selfishness. If any one thing is plain it is that liberalism has been moved by a humanitarian and universalistic impulse.

It is true that historically liberalism has often been associated with materialism, as by the French Encyclopaedists of the Eighteenth Century and by certain German thinkers of the Nineteenth Century. Liberalism has tended to be on the side of natural science whenever, as during the Nineteenth Century, there was an alignment of hostility between science and religion. But neither Locke nor Mill, the two great English proponents of liberalism, was a materialist; and liberalism has had many adherents among philosophical idealists in England and America and on the Continent. Some liberals have been atheists; but it is quite possible to be an atheist without being a liberal, or a liberal without being an atheist. Nor is liberalism, because of its tolerance, either skeptical or unprincipled. As reformer the liberal is dissatisfied with things as they are because they violate his exceptionally tender conscience. Nor does the liberal confuse liberty with license — that is, with the liberty to destroy liberty. He seeks to change or interpret law to make room for greater freedom, but is so wedded to law that he insists on bringing even the lawmaker, whether civil or ecclesiastical, within its jurisdiction. Liberalism does not advocate change for its own sake, but for the sake of something better in the direction of what he regards as good, namely, the maximum of liberty consistent with a regard for all men and all interests — the general happiness based on peace and justice.

That liberalism so defined, or expurgated, has much in common with the Christian gospel needs no argument. If it does not stress the love of God, it does at least embrace the love of neighbor. If it neglects the fatherhood of God, it at any rate proclaims the fraternity of men. If it disparages the church, along with other corporate entities, it is because it is so insistent on the finality of the human person.

The independence of this moral ideal in no sense argues *against* theism. Nor does its independence exalt it above religion. If the Second Great Commandment is independent of the First Great Commandment, it does not follow that the First may not be the higher commandment, provided only that if both are accepted they must be consistent. If the City of Man is autonomous it does not follow

117

that the City of God is not the greater city, provided the laws of the second in no wise transgress the laws of the first.

To say that the ideal of the common happiness has its own appeal to the secular moral will does not imply that a divine sanction would not give it a stronger appeal; or that this reënforcement may not be practically necessary if the ideal is to be realized among men. But if both groups, theistic and non-theistic, were to recognize their adherence to this same ideal they would welcome one another as allies, each reconciling the ideal with its own metaphysical doctrines and working for it with its own symbols and organization.

11

Within the broader dispute concerning liberalism, there arises the sharper issue concerning the separation of church and state. This issue, of such grave concern to America, is not settled by the fact that Catholicism itself distinguishes between church and state; or by the fact that Catholicism is prepared for the present and for an indefinite time to come, to accept the American system. The question remains whether Catholicism agrees in principle with the American idea of a secular state within which every church and sect, Catholicism included, is tolerated.

The liberal doctrine of religious toleration within a secular state began in England and elsewhere in the Sixteenth and Seventeenth Centuries as a consequence of disputes between the several Christian parties, each of which started with the uniformitarian view that its creed should be enforced upon the whole of society through its exclusive rights of propaganda and public worship, and its control of the civil authorities. It became apparent that uniformitarianism led to civil strife, to external conformity and hypocrisy, to the intrusion of the public authority into the personal life, and to the frustration of intellectual and cultural freedom. Men like William of Orange, Cromwell, Milton, and Roger Williams, who were sectarians in their personal beliefs but statesmen in the political sphere, advocated and practiced the idea that the church should be conceived as a private association of men holding a common faith and practicing a common worship, within the public framework of a state that should be primarily occupied with the maintaining of civil order.

This implied no hostility to religion — on the contrary, it was designed to protect religion, and it did as a matter of fact eventually make it possible for the Catholic Church to survive and prosper in communities which were predominantly Protestant. It implied no derogation of the dignity of religion — on the contrary, it sprang in large part from a resentment of the interference of temporal authorities in spiritual matters in which they were deemed incompetent. It did not imply that the saving of souls might not be the most important of all human concerns, but rather that salvation was possible only when spiritual insight was allowed free expression and the way of salvation left open to personal choice. While the liberal state so conceived was secularized, it was not exalted. It was customary to employ the analogy of the company on board a ship who may as individuals possess a higher dignity, and be bent upon more distant errands, but who as fellow-passengers must submit to the captain and obey such rules as are necessary to keep the ship afloat and bring it to port.

The Catholic view of the relations of the church to the secular liberal state, as represented in American democracy, has been made clear. That Catholicism has profited by the liberal principle of religious toleration is fully acknowledged, but with the reservation that ideally the Church cannot be satisfied with being merely tolerated. She would, said Pope Leo XIII, "bring forth more abundant fruits, if, in addition to liberty she enjoyed the favor of the laws, and the patronage of public authority." [25] To quote a Jesuit exponent of the "Leonine" doctrine:

> There is . . . no practical conflict, and no danger of an expressed opposition so long as the United States remains what it has been. The Catholic Church has an ideal of a Christian, Catholic state; that ideal, perhaps, will never be fully expressed in a modern nation, and obviously, never in America. The Church, therefore, in its immemorial practice, adjusting itself to the existing order so long as its divine and human rights are not molested, co-operates in peace with that non-religious, secular order.[26]

In short, the polity which places the Catholic Church on the same plane with other churches or private associations is accepted on opportunistic grounds, and whenever the people of any given society shall be predominantly Catholic the full Leonine doctrine should go into effect. The way of salvation taught by the Catholic Church should then be given unique privileges, and the creed of Catholicism should be the guide of public policy.

The issue has been clouded by misunderstandings and polemical overstatements, but the crux of it is clear. The traditional American doctrine does not imply that all religious cults are on the same plane as regards truth, but only that all *claimants* are on the same plane as members of a *civil society*. The state *as such* here presupposes no truth save the political truth that religious truth is best left to win its way by persuasion and voluntary adherence. It is irrelevant, then, to argue that Catholic Christianity

[25] Encyclical Letter, *Longinque Oceani*, 1895, quoted in C. C. Marshall, *The Roman Catholic Church in the Modern State,* 1931, Appendix II, p. 388.

[26] Rev. Francis X. Talbot, S.J., "Catholicism in America," *America Now,* edited by H. E. Stearns, 1938, p. 539. The Leonine doctrine is set forth in the Encyclical quoted above, and in this Pope's "Christian Constitution of States" (1885) and "Christian Democracy" (*Graves de Communi*) (1901).

is true, and to conclude that error has not the same rights as truth.[27] Such an argument does not in the least affect the liberalistic contention that rival sectaries should have the same civil rights. It is an indisputable fact that Catholicism *is* a religious sect, regardless of truth or error. It is a fact admitted in any history of religions which defines the peculiar tenets of Catholicism, any religious census which states the amount of its property, or the number of its adherents. The view of secular liberalism is that for *political* purposes Catholicism is to be so construed, as one of several sects, and that for the good of mankind in general and for the good of each and every sect, including Catholicism, sectarian differences should be settled by discussion and not by political action.

That there is here a conflict, or the seed of a conflict, must be regretfully concluded. Catholicism, it is true, recognizes the advantages which the Church enjoys under American institutions — its freedom from persecution, its immunity from interference by government, its opportunity to practice and profess its faith and to gain adherents. But the distinctive ideas of a cult are not to be found in the tactics which it adopts when it is a minority. All minorities, whether Christian or Buddhist, theist or atheist, Communist or Fascist, Protestant or Catholic, desire to be tolerated. Religious cults ordinarily seek to transform their

27 This is the argument used by Pope Leo XIII: "Men have a right freely and prudently to propagate throughout the State what things soever are true and honorable, so that as many as possible may possess them; but lying opinions, than which no mental plague is greater, and vices which corrupt the heart and moral life, should be diligently repressed by public authority, lest they insidiously work the ruin of the State. The excesses of an unbridled intellect, which unfailingly end in the oppression of the untutored multitude, are no less rightly controlled by the authority of the law than are the injuries inflicted by violence upon the weak." Encyclical Letter, *Libertas praestantissimum*, June 20, 1888, reprinted in J. A. Ryan and F. J. Boland, *Catholic Principles of Politics*, 1940, pp. 174–5.

minority into a majority or a unanimity. In the realm of ideas and ideals, therefore, a cult is to be distinguished by its hope — by its conception of that hour of triumph to which its members look forward, however remotely, and with whatever degree of doubt or confidence. And it cannot be said that the American hope and the Catholic hope are the same, since Americans hope for an increased degree of tolerance and freedom, whereas Catholics appear to hope for an increased degree of uniformitarian control — for that, namely, which the settlers of America came to America to escape.

Meanwhile, there is danger of conflict between Americanism and Catholicism within each individual Catholic's breast. His Americanism inclines him to personal independence and self-reliance — to a making up of his own mind, to a free interchange of ideas, to a spirit of criticism and inquiry, and to voluntary, rather than submissive, agreement. His Catholicism, on the other hand, inclines him to the acceptance, or to the imposing, of authority.

This difficulty is not escaped by the limitation of authority to a restricted area, because, in the first place, the habit or attitude of unquestioning obedience, once implanted, is likely to spread to all areas of opinion and action; and because, in the second place, the definition of the limits of the Church's authority itself lies within the area of the Church's authority.

12

The reconciliation of Catholicism and Americanism is to be sought in their common adherence to that ideal of the "common happiness"; which has the sanction of Thomas Aquinas, as well as of Protestantism, Judaism, and secular liberalism. The sharing of this ideal would not imply that it was the supreme ideal: some might believe that it was supreme, being the latest and highest phase of man's ascent from physical nature; while others might believe that, to use the words of Pope Pius XI, "in this world and in the next, man has no last end save God." [28] To some the terrestrial, temporal, and natural would be all, and to others these would be supplemented and crowned by the celestial, eternal, and supernatural. Or, to use a simile of Jacques Maritain,[29] it would mean that the horizontal plane was the same for two or more vertical foundations or superstructures. Citizenship in the City of Man would for some constitute the only citizenship, while for others it would be supplemented and consummated by a higher citizenship in the City of God.

At least in the area of action, there appears to be no insuperable Catholic objection to such reconciliation. The Catholic Association for International Peace has recently published a pamphlet on *Intercredal Coöperation*. After summarizing papal utterances on "the progress and happiness of the whole family," this pamphlet concludes that this goal can be achieved only by a united effort embracing non-Catholics as well as Catholics — "all men of good will," "all those who are upright of heart,". . ."innumerable souls of good will," "the other millions of sincere souls," "all men of good faith," "all those who glory in the name of Christians," "multitudes of just souls, even those alien to the Catholic faith."

It is not entirely clear that this alliance for the common temporal good is to include those who disbelieve in God. Good will is construed as a sort of nascent piety: the issue is one between those who are for, and those who are against, God; the bond unites those "who acknowledge God and with sincere hearts adore Him." On the other hand, the program is motivated by the sentiment of char-

---

[28] *Divini Redemptoris*, 1937, par. 27; quoted by Rev. John J. Wright, *National Patriotism in Papal Teaching*, 1942, p. xxvii.

[29] Cf. this writer's "Christian Humanism," *Fortune*, April, 1942.

ity and deduced from the natural and moral law, so that it would seem that the possession of a tender and enlightened conscience would be a sufficient qualification for participation.[30]

In entering upon such an agreement the Catholic would reserve not only his peculiar dogmas, but his hope of eventually converting all men of good will to their acceptance. He would acknowledge the civil legitimacy of a similar hope on the part of other groups. Beyond the common civil and social code there would be a recognized right to differ — an agreement to agree, and an agreement to disagree.

If one were to draw up the reckoning at the present time, it would be somewhat as follows. Catholicism is uncongenial to Americanism in its authoritarianism, and in the passive obedience which this implies; in its basing of civil polity and secular morality on specific religious doctrines, attributed to revelation and involving a supernaturalistic metaphysics; in its claim of doctrinal infallibility; in its ultimate uniformitarian goal; in its disposition to use the agencies of the state for the promotion of a specific religious creed and worship.

Catholicism, together with Protestantism and Judaism, is congenial to Americanism, on the other hand, in its insistence on the priority of moral principles to the civil law and to the authority of the state; in its emphasis on the irreducible worth of the individual person; in its exaltation of the motives of love and compassion; in its subordination of individual selfishness to the good of the community as a whole, and of national selfishness to the good of mankind at large; in its faith in moral progress; in its recognition of a fundamental human equality which eclipses differences of racial, social, political, or economic status.

[30] Wilfred Parsons and J. C. Murray, *Intercredal Coöperation*, Washington, 1943, pp. 6, 10, 12–13, 28, 34.

The American Religious Heritage

The crux of the issue between Americanism and religion of any description, is tolerance, this being taken as a principle, and not as a mere expedient: Americanism implies that saving doubt — that "perhaps" — which softens the inquisitorial temper; that intellectual humility which stops men from imposing exclusive opinions by force or by indoctrination; that faith in general truth which is fearless of the discussion of particular questions; that spirit of discovery and openness toward the future, that recognition of boundless possibilities, which shrinks from narrow and rigid commitments; that respect of a man for his fellows which, whatever his office or title, and even though he speaks in the name of God, forbids his treating them as children, minors or dependents.

The discouragements of the present age incline men to the acceptance of authority, and to the surrender of individuality. The hour is therefore propitious to any institution which offers men certitude, and which embraces them within a corporate entity to which they can entrust their fortunes. But to accept the decrees of authority — an authority of person or of office — can scarcely be the last word of man's emancipated intellect; to belong to, and be possessed by, a being other than himself can scarcely be the last word of man's self-conscious and self-directing personality. There is another way, the American way, which combines self-reliance with benevolence, individual effort with coöperation, and a candid recognition of the facts and admission of past failures with present conviction and faith in the future.

V

American Democracy

1

THERE ARE MANY DEMOCRACIES: ancient democracy and modern democracy; Eighteenth Century democracy and Nineteenth Century democracy; Jeffersonian democracy and Jacksonian democracy; Eastern democracy and Western democracy; political democracy and social democracy; democracy in theory and democracy in practice. In short, democracy means so many things as to raise doubts of its meaning anything at all. One meaning, however, it certainly has, namely, an "emotive meaning" — for Americans.[1] Candidates for office in America are unlikely to arise and proclaim their disbelief in democracy. American foreign policy wins popular support through raising the banner of democracy in the world at large and associating America with other "democracies." In short, the word "democracy" has an appeal to Americans. Americans are for it, whatever it means.

While granting that the vocabulary of democracy has acquired an emotive meaning among Americans, it also has a "descriptive" or "objective" meaning; that is, it refers to a certain form of social organization, which serves as a norm of criticism and guiding principle of reform. If this vocabulary did not have a descriptive or objective meaning, it would be impossible to explain its emotive meaning, since the latter is a degeneration of the former; as the

[1] This expression derives its current vogue among philosophers largely from C. L. Stevenson's *Ethics and Language,* 1944, *q.v. passim.*

Mother's Day meaning of the term "mother," would be inexplicable without the actual biological relationship from which it has arisen.

It is quite true that a campaign speech of which nothing was audible save such words as "democracy," "freedom," "liberty," "equality," "rights," and "the people," repeated at intervals with the right intonation and emphasis, would be received with thunderous applause. But unless these terms were directly or indirectly associated in men's minds with certain social conditions, it would not be possible to trace the genesis of their emotional appeal. Their rhetorical spell once acquired can be cast by the bare words, but only because they were once the names for certain ideas, and in reflective moods will still bring these to mind. It is quite true that the word "mother," properly intoned, has a tear-jerking power of its own; but this fact cannot be used as an argument for asexual reproduction, or against the existence of filial and maternal instincts.

The basic idea which gives to the word "democracy" its original and latent meaning is the idea of a social group organized and directed by all of its members for the benefit of all of its members. It may be contended that such an organization has never existed in human history; that actual human societies have, as a matter of fact, come into being without conscious intent, as a result of instinct, habit, or force; that they have been directed by some of their members to the exclusion of others; and that their benefits have been enjoyed by a privileged fraction of the whole. But this does not prevent the entertainment of the idea taken as an ideal, approximated more or less closely in human history, and occasionally realized on a small scale and under peculiarly favorable conditions.

There are several common misunderstandings which need to be noted and corrected at the outset: the confusion of the people with the "masses," the confusion of the people with the majority, and the supposed antithesis of democracy to republicanism.

The confusion of the people with the "masses," arises from the fact that at any given time the idea of democracy requires the rectification of existing inequalities. Throughout the greater part of human history societies have been pyramidal in structure, with a concentration of power and benefits at the apex. Hence the idea of democracy ordinarily requires that power and benefits shall be given to the more numerous class, and, if need be, taken away from the less numerous class. But the more numerous class has enjoyed a more restricted opportunity of personal development, and is largely motivated by resentment. Hence the term "masses" means not merely the more numerous but the ignorant, primitive, covetous, embittered; and the democratic movement is conceived not only as horizontally enlarging, but as vertically debasing. This, however, is not the *idea* of democracy; which would be better fulfilled if the more numerous class were leveled up, or were thought of not in terms of their defects, but in terms of those merits, such as industry, sagacity, and plainness of living, which have given rise to the notion of the "common man."

Similarly, the identification of the people with the majority is of the accident rather than of the essence of democracy. Ideally democracy implies an agreement of all parties, reached by a pooling of their interests, and a sharing of their wisdom. Owing, however, to the conflict of interests, and the imperfections of human wisdom, complete agreement cannot be reached in time to meet the date-line of action. It is necessary to accept the decision of the majority as a provisional substitute for unanimity. There is an agreement of all parties to accept a partial agreement, as representing the nearest approximation to total agreement that is practically possible; assuming that dissenters will eventually be persuaded, or will in their turn prevail.

Meanwhile, the minority retains its constitutional rights, as a protection against exploitation, and as affording an opportunity of becoming a majority.

There are those who insist, alluding to the Founding Fathers, that America is a "republic," and *not* a democracy. That America is a republic is beyond dispute, and this term also has its favorable emotive meaning. But the difference between the two ideas is one of degree and not of kind. It turns on the fact that all modern democracies, with local or occasional exceptions, such as the town-meeting and the referendum, are representative democracies. The people govern more or less indirectly, the popular mandate is given more or less frequently, and elected representatives are allowed more or less discretion, depending on the confidence reposed in the political judgment of the rank and file of mankind. Those who prefer "republic" to "democracy" are those who, being relatively doubtful of average human capacity and fearful of demagogues, put greater trust in supposedly superior persons who have been chosen by the people to act for them.

The term "republic" may also be used for a polity in which the people are protected from the effects of their own hasty judgment, or in which individuals and minorities are protected against momentary majorities, by a constitution which divides and limits the powers of government, and which can be changed only by some relatively slow and laborious process of amendment. The term "democracy" will be used in the present context interchangeably with the term "republic" to mean a representative political system in which the people rule more or less directly, and with more or less constitutional restraint.

2

Democracy consists of two distinct but interdependent parts, which it will be convenient to designate as political and social democracy. Political democracy concerns the question of control, and affirms that it shall be exercised by the people at large; social democracy concerns the question of benefits, and affirms that they shall be enjoyed by the people at large. Integral democracy, in which these two parts are united, is society controlled by the people at large for their own benefit; those who rule are the same as those who benefit; each individual, or "citizen," by virtue of being one of the people plays a double rôle, as one who shares both the power and the profit.

These two parts of democracy are interdependent. Political power is itself a benefit, since men desire power, and are designed by their human faculties to exercise it. Benefits confer power, since the extent of the individual's power will reflect the educational and economic advantages which he enjoys. As a consequence of benefits enjoyed, the people will be qualified to direct their own affairs; and as a consequence of directing their own affairs they will confer benefits upon themselves. Hence integral democracy will be a benign circle, in which the political and social factors are alike both cause and effect.

The political and social aspects of democracy need not advance abreast. As a matter of fact, democracy usually moves askew. The impulse of democracy at any given time is applied to the backward part, which is then easily mistaken for the whole. Or, given a non-democratic society, in which popular impotence begets exploitation, and exploitation in turn begets impotence, the vicious circle may be broken at either point. A non-democratic government may relieve the exploited, and by distributing benefits more widely, fit the people to manage their own affairs; or the people by acquiring power may secure for themselves a greater part of the proceeds. Hence it may happen that two societies may both claim to be adherents of democracy, and rightly so, when they are out of step. This is one of the reasons why the United States, which places its democratic emphasis on popular government and condemns the authoritarian state, finds it so difficult to understand how the term "democracy" can be employed by those societies, such as Soviet Russia, whose primary concern is the deliverance of workers and peasants from economic exploitation, and are comparatively indifferent to the political means by which this end is sought.

3

The political history of the United States, broadly surveyed, is a record of increasing popular self-government. The so-called "American Revolution" was a revolution in a doubly limited sense. It was primarily a political and not a social revolution; and as a political revolution it was external rather than internal. It was an act of separation, by which a group of colonies became a self-governing state. At the same time feudalism, monarchism, and hereditary aristocracy were left behind on the other side of the water, and did not need to be overthrown by civil revolt. The act of separation left standing the representative legislatures of the colonies, and the governors appointed from abroad were replaced by governors elected at home.

This initial accent on political rather than social revolution, and on external rather than internal political revolution, has left a durable imprint on the American democratic attitude, seen in its emphasis on "self-determination," and in the traditional American sympathy with every effort of a colony, or conquered people, or backward area, whether in South America, or in Hungary, Poland, or India, to throw off imperial control and achieve a government of its own.

It is significant, therefore, that the American democratic charter should be named "The Declaration of *Independence*." It is also significant that there should have been a *"Declaration."* The principles which it embraced were not novel, but were part of the British inheritance and were shared with the contemporary European world. That which was characteristically American was the solemn profession of these principles, and the extent to which their application was unhindered by relics of the undemocratic past. America was afforded an unparalleled opportunity of building a democracy on cleared ground and with fit materials; not only with abundant natural resources, but with a population disposed to democracy by the self-reliant temper of uprooted pioneers.

Hence America realized the democratic idea in advance of the European countries in which the idea had originated. The steps of this advance are well-known: [2] the removal of restrictions on suffrage, the free admission of residents to citizenship and of newly settled regions to statehood, the separation of church and state, the widening circle of those who were politically conscious and eligible for office, the popular election of president and senators, the increased use of the initiative and referendum, the quickened response of officials to the opinion of constituents. Great presidents, without amendment of their constitutional function, have learned how to appeal directly to the people over the head of Congress, and how to appeal to the whole people against the resistance of special interests and localities. Even the Supreme Court has become increasingly responsive to public opinion.

All of these political developments may be said to move

2 Cf. Francis Lieber, *On Civil Liberty and Self-Government*, 1853, Vol. I, pp. 277–86.

away from John Adams and in the direction of Thomas Jefferson. The latter, it is true, contemplated a rural rather than an urban and industrialized society; but he put his trust in the people at large rather than in the upper stratum of wealth and position which at any given time had enjoyed superior advantages. He believed in two aristocracies, the aristocracy of talent and the aristocracy of virtue. The former he thought to be distributed among all classes of society, and the latter he thought should be open to all men through education. Neither of these aristocracies coincided either actually or ideally with the aristocracy of birth and position.

The view of Adams was admirably summarized by Chancellor James Kent, who found the worst fears of the Federalists to be justified by Jacksonian democracy:

> The tendency of universal suffrage is to jeopardize the rights of property, and the principles of liberty. There is a constant tendency in human society, and the history of every age proves it; there is a tendency in the poor to covet a share in the plunder of the rich; in the debtor to relax or avoid the obligation of contracts; in the majority to tyrannize over the minority, and trample down their rights; in the indolent and profligate, to cast the whole burthens of society upon the industrious and the virtuous; and *there is a tendency in ambitious and wicked men, to inflame these combustible materials.*[3]

It will be noted that Chancellor Kent identified virtue, industry, and the keeping of contracts with wealth; that he says nothing of the tyranny of the minority over the majority; nor of the ambitious and wicked men who hire the demagogues, and thus direct government to the ends of a privileged class. By slight verbal amendments his statement could be made to express the opposing fears, the Jeffer-

---

[3] *Reports of the Proceedings and Debates of the N.Y. Constitutional Convention of 1821;* quoted by H. R. Warfel (ed.) , *The American Mind,* 1937, Vol. I, pp. 261–2.

sonian-Jacksonian fears, which have in the long run prevailed.

The Civil War was complexly motivated. It was "a war between the states," and a war against slavery, but above all, and in Lincoln's mind, it was a war for the preservation of the Union — a war in the name of all against a segment, and a war in the name of the American people against the independent sovereignties of states. It marked the birth of a new spirit of nationalism, in which the people of the United States were re-dedicated to the principles of the Declaration of Independence, and felt a new sense of solidarity and forward movement.

4

With the emphasis on political democracy in the early years of American development was associated the idea of the limited rôle of government. The seeming paradox is, however, entirely explicable. The American Revolution was a rejection of the government of the British Parliament and Crown — a "dissolving of bands" — and government acquired evil associations from that fact. Furthermore, the American people, for divers and evident reasons, felt that they were quite competent to look out for their own happiness if only they were let alone to do it, and that government could best serve their happiness by seeing to it that they *were* let alone. Government was designed to afford the maximum of free-play to those motives and forces by which self-reliant individuals carve out their own fortunes.

This view was peculiarly plausible when the typical American was the independent hunter, miner, or small subsistence farmer. Crêvecoeur, writing in 1782, described Americans as "cultivators" who worked for themselves, and

exhibited "a pleasing uniformity of decent competence." [4]
Fifty years later Washington Irving could still feel a nostalgia for that state of man in which the individual was competent to provide for his modest wants with the labor of his own hands:

> Such is the glorious independence of man in a savage state. This youth, with his rifle, his blanket, and his horse, was ready at a moment's warning to rove the world; he carried all his worldly effects with him, and in the absence of artificial wants possessed the great secret of personal freedom. We of society are slaves, not so much to others, as to ourselves; our superfluities are the chains that bind us, impeding every movement of our bodies and thwarting every impulse of our souls. [5]

This idyllic condition, if, indeed it has ever existed save in the literary imagination, has long since ceased to be characteristic of American life. Here America has followed the way of Hamilton, and become a vast industrial complex, providing by an intricate division of labor, and by improved technology for an ever multiplying and more insistent set of wants. The problem of social democracy in America is to reconcile with this all-pervading interdependence the Jeffersonian ideas of equality, freedom, and personal dignity.

The same problem arose from the laissez-faire economy, according to which the individual could achieve wealth, and all that wealth could bring, by his private initiative and energy. At the same time, so it was argued, or assumed, society at large was benefited, and protected against the inordinate selfishness of an individual or group, by the widely diffused effects of invention, ambition, increased production, and competition. The development of social

[4] Hector St. John de Crèvecoeur, Letter III of his *Letters from an American Farmer*, 1783, p. 47.
[5] Washington Irving, *A Tour on the Prairies*, 1835, pp. 42-3.

democracy in America is best understood as a series of withdrawals from this too optimistic doctrine.

For from the beginning of the Industrial Revolution it was apparent that its blessings were mixed. It led to urban congestion, unhealthy living and working conditions, excessive hours of labor for women and children as well as for men, and a bare subsistence wage. And from the beginning it was found necessary that the conscience of society should intervene to protect the public against the evil effects of private greed. This conscience had various organs of expression: the protests of reformers, such as the early socialists; the churches, Protestant and Catholic; the workers themselves, and their trade unions; but ultimately the government, conceived as the agency whose business it is to promote the good of all against, if necessary, the special interest of a few.

The first phase of this social democratic force took the form of ameliorative legislation. But in the course of time the emphasis shifted. It became increasingly evident that laissez-faire capitalism tended, as it developed, to defeat that general good by which it was defended, and even to defeat itself. Unrestricted competition tended to monopoly, since the surest and most final way to outstrip a competitor is to destroy him. Large-scale industry led to vast accumulations of private capital and to the control of industry by finance, to uninvested savings, to the production of luxuries rather than necessities, and to the creation of a private economic power which rivaled or controlled the power of the state.

Meanwhile, the individual became increasingly dependent on a complicated, widely ramifying, and closely knit economic system over which he had little or no control. The worker was, it is true, free to withhold his labor, but only at the peril of his life. Wages, conceived as a major cost of production, tended to be depressed. Workers were employed en masse in congested and stagnant pools, and found it increasingly difficult to lift themselves from their surroundings. Their individual helplessness gave them a solidarity of interest which found expression in ever bigger and better unions, directed against rapacious or complacent employers, who organized in their turn. Both parties became increasingly class-conscious. There remained only one agency, namely government, which owed allegiance to neither class, and which was, or could be, powerful enough to deal with them both.

Hence the increasing tendency of government to intervene in business — to regulate, or even control. The high-water mark of this tendency was the New Deal, which, however, was new neither in theory nor in practice, but only in the degree to which it asserted the duty of organized society to look to the welfare of all of its members. It represented the impulse of social democracy in the direction of its own inherent meaning, and under changed conditions. Public education and public health, old-age, disability, and unemployment benefits, a minimum wage, organized labor and collective bargaining, government works, the regulation, or even the nationalization, of certain industries, are not to be considered as heresies, or as importations of alien ideologies, but as applications of the American democratic principle that it is the business of government, speaking for all the people, to promote their good as may fit the circumstances.

5

In the discussion of American democracy, political and social, the word "people" has hitherto been employed, with the usual carelessness and with the usual unction; as when the surprising election of 1948 was said to signify that "the people" had spoken. "People," too, is a word having a rhetorical value which tends to obscure its objective meaning, and to evade the profound difficulties which the idea entails. Just how popular opinion and sentiment are actually created in America remains a mystery. It has become clear that they are not the product of any single "force," and that they cannot be "scientifically" predicted. But it is possible to state what is implied in the *idea* of democracy.

In theory "the people" signifies an aggregate of individuals who agree, that is, who judge and will the same. Since such agreement does not exist *ab initio,* it has to be achieved; and it is the democratic idea that it should be achieved not by force, nor by habit, nor by emotional contagion, but by discussion. Democracy is opposed in principle to the use of violence, not primarily because it is destructive, but because, whatever its outcome, it is a failure to agree. Evolution, when opposed to revolution, signifies an agreement won by peaceful persuasion.

The model of the people, in the democratic sense, is to be found in small groups of persons who, being animated by a desire to agree, interchange opinions and take account of one another's interests: so that in the end it is possible for each person to use the plural pronoun "we," and not merely the singular pronoun "I." Since, however, no national society *is* a small group, differences of judgment and interest will always remain. The most that can be hoped for is an agreement to disagree in an orderly manner; or acquiescence to a general plan, in which more specific disagreements can be tolerated, and in which, when collective action is required, there can be a temporary preponderant opinion, postponing the settlement of residual disagreements.

The popular judgment and will, so construed, require that each individual shall not only assert his own interest and opinion, but shall be receptive to the interests and opinions of others; that is, shall in some measure be governed by what is called "good will," "social consciousness," or "public spirit." Whatever works against this spirit works against democracy. There are two such anti-democratic forces whose growth must be of grave concern to any friend of American democracy.

The first of these is the original sin of selfishness, aggravated by the self-seeking and self-assertiveness characteristic of Americans and sanctioned by their competitive economy. Selfishness may govern the individual or the special interest of a class or locality. In either case the policy which it dictates may or may not coincide with the general interest. It is a common error to suppose that the truth necessarily emerges from a multiplicity or clash of opposing opinions; which may produce only confusion, clamor, and a hardening of differences. Discussion promotes truth only when different minds listen to one another, and assist one another to consider the common evidence. Similarly, community of interests does not emerge from the mere insistence of each on itself, but requires sympathy. If there is to be a good of all, a general happiness, each individual must be imaginatively sensitive to desires, needs, and wants which he does not originally feel as his own.

This capacity is not a fictitious invention of sentimentalists. The simplest forms of coöperation would be impossible could a man not enlarge his will to embrace another's, resolving both into a common purpose served by both alike. Nor is this community of purpose to be confused with that subtle, or so-called "enlightened," selfishness in which the will of another is served as a means to one's own pre-existing will. In true community of purpose, whether defined as an ideal, or partially achieved in human practice, the ends of both parties are united in a new end in which both participate.

Government is called upon to make every interest its

own: it must be disinterested, in the sense of all-interested.
This it fails to do in proportion as it merely duplicates the
conflicting interests of its constituents. If Congress is lowly
esteemed in America it is primarily because it leaves to the
Executive, or to the comparative high-mindedness of a few
of its members, the heavy task of reconciling interests. And
if democracy is to fulfil its meaning, this high-mindedness
or disinterestedness must be widely diffused not only
among the officials of government, but among the members of society at large, in order that they may supplement
their private concerns with a concern for all. This places
a heavy burden on the educational processes by which individuals must be taught to play the rôle of citizens.

The second of the forces which works against the creation of a people which shall meet the requirements of democracy, is the vulgarization of sentiment and opinion.
Like selfishness, this anti-democratic force has always existed, and has always been recognized by social philosophers. And this force, also, is aggravated in America both by
national characteristics and by the tendencies of the modern age.

Americans do not easily accept authority from above,
but they are highly vulnerable to the impersonal and unorganized authority of their social environment. It is not
a vertical uniformity which America has reason to fear,
but a horizontal uniformity — a mere spread from next to
next.

This tendency to mass uniformity is strongly reënforced
by the modern techniques of mass-communication. The
press and radio seek that wide attention which is the condition of their commercial success by providing suitable
stimuli to reflexes, instincts, habits, and prevailing emotional attitudes. If for any combination of reasons large
numbers of people are moved by fear or rage, their attention is attracted by that which caters to their fear and rage.

If a cliché or slogan has obtained wide currency, the most widespread and effortless response is evoked by its repetition. In order to create the mentality of a crowd or mob it was once necessary that a large aggregate of persons should be gathered in one spot; now it is only necessary that they shall read the same headlines or listen to the same news commentator. Space and time once worked against mass-contagion, or held it within bounds; now a whole people, spread over half a continent, can be emotionally inflamed or instantly converted to the same opinion.

American like-mindedness suffers not from lack of likeness, but from lack of mind. The danger is not that men shall think differently, but that they shall not think at all; not that they shall feel differently, but that their feeling shall lack maturity and depth. A major portion of American thought is devoted to creating substitutes for thought; the deepest feeling is excited by the invention of new techniques for exciting shallow feeling. Ideas and sentiments have become packaged commodities, produced and distributed in mass, and designed for mass-consumption.

Here, then, is the gravest of problems for American democracy in the modern age — how to create a popular will that shall harmonize conflicting interests, and a public opinion that shall reflect a thoughtful agreement. At the same time that special interests are divided and opposed, and the American mind is vulnerable to the commercialized techniques of mass-communication, the American people are called upon to play the leading part in world affairs, and the American citizen is required to pass judgment on economic and international questions of growing complexity.

In some measure this problem is met by the hundreds and thousands of small groups, in which private citizens meet for the discussion of public problems and, having reached agreement, exert influence upon the government or upon their fellow-citizens at large. Having spoken of the earlier town-meeting, Frances Perkins writes:

> The lineal descendants of those groups . . . were the discussion clubs, the leagues, the circles, the associations connected with the colleges and the churches — all the centers where people met to talk things over together. . . . These discussion centers are the actual birth places of public opinion — they are where the American mind, harnessed to the American will, goes constructively and critically to work.[6]

These groups and organizations not only create nuclei of agreement, but develop among their members and disseminate to others a spirit of fair-mindedness and civic responsibility.

There is hope also in a growing awareness of their public obligations on the part of the press, radio, and other agencies of mass-communication, and in their increasing self-criticism. But in the end American democracy must rely most on the long-range effects of education. The so-called "educated," who have enjoyed the advantages of formal schooling, must start in life with some understanding of the forces which, during their later lives, will mould their minds. As things stand at present even the graduates of universities are scarcely less vulnerable to the appeal of selfish interests and to the making of the tabloid mind, than their less privileged fellow-citizens.

6

The meaning of American democracy can be approached through the idea of freedom. The emotional value of the word "freedom" has throughout American history probably exceeded that of any other word, even "democracy" or "people." Judging by recent campaign

6 *People at Work*, 1934, p. 37.

oratory, this is a word that gets votes, or, at any rate, applause. In Governor Dewey's brief speech accepting the Republican nomination, the words "free" and "freedom" occurred twenty times — not counting their opposites, or their equivalents, such as "liberty." In the present grave crisis between the American and Soviet spheres of influence, Americans are eager to regard themselves as the champions of what they call "freedom" against its enemies.

The appeal of the word "freedom" arises not only from traditional symbolism and verbal habits, but from the fact that it arouses the combative instincts and flatters the ego. It also possesses a meaning which every man can translate into terms of his own experience. Every man is afflicted with something he would like to be free *from*. There are as many freedoms as there are constraints to be escaped; and the general cult of freedom is a sort of blank check which each man fills out for himself in terms of those particular circumstances whose constraint he feels. Freedom becomes a conscious good which men prize and seek only when there is this feeling of confinement, this pressing against some barrier and sense of its opposing force.

Since there are many freedoms, the freedom of one person will differ from that of another, and the meaning of freedom will differ from age to age. One man's freedom may be another's bondage, and the instruments of one freedom may abridge another. Life is largely a choice between one yoke, and another by which it escapes the first.[7]

There are many variables of which the experience of freedom is compounded. Thus it reflects both the strength of the will and the strength of that which opposes the will. One does not feel pinned down unless one tries to move, or balked unless one is making an effort. Neither the

---

[7] For a penetrating and ironical description of the dilemma of the liberal who to escape economic tyranny surrenders his individual liberty to the state, cf. Carl L. Becker, *Everyman His Own Historian*, 1935.

apathetic man nor the man who is presented with insuperable obstacles will have much sense of freedom. A vivid sense of freedom will arise when a strong will meets a yielding environment. Or freedom may reflect the fact that desires have been so curtailed as to fit the environment. Freedom may be experienced by the individual, as when we speak of "personal freedom"; or by an aggregate of individuals, as when we speak of the freedom of a group or nation. Freedom is limited by the physical environment, as when we speak of man's dependence on nature; or by the social environment.

The constraining force of society may be a public institution, such as government, or it may spring from other private individuals, organized or unorganized. Men would not have suffered the constraint of government had they not first suffered from the greed and violence of their fellows. Slavery, which symbolizes the extremest lack of freedom, has as a rule been a private and not a public institution, and the remedy has been found in government's suppressing the freedom of the slave-holder. Southern slave-holders became the fierce advocates of the freedom of states in order that they might be free to deny freedom to their slaves.

Freedom may be curtailed not only from without, but from within, as when a man is enslaved by one of his own appetites or habits. And finally, freedom may be restricted not only by the presence of a constraining force but by the absence of necessary instruments and resources; as when the handicapped feel, and are judged to be, unfree.

The meaning of freedom to Americans is a mixture of all of these motives. The "land of the free and the home of the brave" is a land of which the inhabitants have been delivered, by their removal to a distance, and by their courageous act of revolt, from the yoke of the British government; and they propose to maintain such independence. They claim, and to some extent enjoy, freedom from the excessive control of their own government. They are characterized by a certain degree of lawlessness, or "take the law into their own hands." They are, or at least were for a time, comparatively free from interference by one another, owing to their mobility and the spaciousness of their domain. At the same time, being high-spirited and self-assertive, Americans are keenly aware of that which is for them or against them. They have possessed and still possess rich resources, both natural resources, and personal or social opportunity. They "value freedom" because they are confident that they can make use of resources and seize opportunities.

The conflict of freedoms and their shifting emphasis in America is illustrated by the interaction of private and institutional freedoms. The freedom first emphasized by Americans was freedom from government — first, freedom from alien government in order to enjoy a government of their own, then, freedom from their own in order to be unhampered in their pursuit of wealth. But freedom developed new private enemies. The worker felt a bondage to the employer, or to the owner of the capital on which his livelihood depended. The unprivileged felt themselves crushed by poverty and disability or by their helplessness to rise above the social condition into which they were born. Small business felt the yoke of big business, and all parties felt the yoke of monopolistic control. Thus in the name of freedom men turned for relief to government, judging its yoke to be the milder of the two. Whereupon government again became the foremost enemy of freedom in the minds of those persons who in the absence of government had been the oppressors rather than the oppressed, who had no fear of their own privation, and whose primary concern, in the name of "free enterprise," was to be allowed to do business for themselves. Those who advocated freedom *from* government, and those who advocated freedom *by* government — Herbert Hoover and Franklin D. Roosevelt — both spoke in the name of freedom. Both opposed regimentation, but they found it in different places; the one in social and economic legislation, the other in the concentration of economic power. There was, and there still remains, a choice between freedom from the TVA and freedom from the Commonwealth and Southern, or between freedom from Washington and freedom from Wall Street.

7

Among the freedoms which are most talked about by Americans at the present time is freedom of thought, including expression, communication, and assembly; that is, the freedom to make up one's own mind and then to persuade other minds to accept one's conclusions. These are by no means the only freedoms which are comprised under the expression "civil liberties," or that are embraced within the traditional bills of rights; but they are now so greatly jeopardized by the power of propaganda, censorship, and inquisition, that in the minds of many Americans they are taken to constitute the whole of freedom or even the whole of democracy.

It is essential to the meaning of political democracy that political authority should rest upon the freely formed judgment of those who are called upon to obey it. This principle is violated in so far as government itself, by intimidation, by education, or by a control of the agencies of publicity, creates the popular judgment by which it then justifies its authority. A democratic government, at least in times of peace, has no business with the minds of its people except as it may enable them to think and speak for themselves — short of incitements to violence. "Totalitarianism" is now the name commonly given to the enemies of democracy — to Communism, as well as to Fascism and Nazism; and Totalitarianism, when it means anything, means a forced, or drugged, or indoctrinated uniformity of belief and imagination by which government obtains a specious consent to its own autocratic policies. It prevents or stifles independent-mindedness in the arts and sciences as well as in the political forum.

While there is no doubt where American democracy stands in principle, there is some doubt as to where it stands in practice and in the attitude of the average man. There are a great many Americans who, after several centuries of professing tolerance, still think that freedom of thought begins and ends with their own thinking, or that it should be limited to those who think "the truth." Americans are also likely to forget that the freedom to think is prized by those who have the leisure, the desire, and the capacity to think; and that its value may not be appreciated by those who are primarily concerned with the freedom to survive. It might even with some plausibility be contended that those who assert the right to think for themselves do not really desire to think, but only to assert the opinions which they have borrowed from others. Finally, it is to be noted that there is a rivalry between this freedom and others; and that those who are outraged by the denial of their freedom to fix the price of butter or beefsteak may be quite indifferent to the denial of the freedom to think, especially if it be somebody else's freedom to think that the price of butter and beefsteak should be regulated by government. Those who oppose socialism in the name of "free enterprise" are likely to forget that thinking itself is a free enterprise; and that the socialist, even though he proposes to curtail the freedom of private business, in advocating such a proposal is demanding the freedom to advocate it.

These considerations are not argued against the prin-

147

ciple of freedom, but only against such limited applications of the principle as may suit some special interest or partial view of the complexities of life. The principle of freedom requires the taking account of many freedoms, the recognition of their conflicts, and the attempt to arrive at the greatest total freedom.

8

Freedom to think is not merely a special freedom. It underlies all other freedoms. It is true that the term "freedom" may be used to signify a mere release of impulse; as when hunger, for example, is associated with the presence of food, the absence of impediments, and the presence of the reflexes of grasping and swallowing. When, however, we speak of freedom as a distinctively human good, sought or possessed by persons, it implies choice. A man is free in proportion as he does what he chooses. Freedom in this human and personal sense requires the *capacity* to choose.

It is the self which chooses, and in order that there may be a self to make a choice, it is necessary that the several impulses which move the individual shall be integrated in a total or reflective will. In proportion as an individual lacks such a reflective will, and remains a mere complex of impulses, each in turn excluding the rest, he does not choose, because there is no "he." The personal pronoun has as yet achieved no meaning beyond that of a physical organism. The proper pronoun would be "it"; as in the case of vegetables and lower animals. The personal pronouns imply some degree of self-consciousness, some drawing of impulses to a common center, some thinking over of each in relation to the rest.

But this is not all that is implied in choice. It is further necessary that this self or personal will shall be aware of alternatives. There is no choosing without a choosing of

148

this rather than that, and the degree of freedom is proportional to the range of possibilities with which the choosing person is consciously confronted; which implies not only imagination, but knowledge of real, as distinguished from merely imaginary, possibilities.

The capacity for freedom links man's other social institutions with education, and throws light on what education for democracy requires. It comprises a knowledge of the facts of life, and of the means by which the will is made effectual — the tools, the instruments, the causal relations, which condition achievement. In so far as such knowledge is general rather than specific, it equips the individual for constructive originality, and prepares him for a variety of later choices, without premature commitment.

Education is "liberal" in proportion as it assists in the formation of a personal will, develops the faculty of choice, and furnishes that faculty with a rich reservoir of estimated possibilities. It enables the individual to choose for himself, circumspectly and wisely. It is opposed to such education as merely fits the individual for a form of activity that is chosen for him by others, or is the result of circumstances beyond his control. Ideally it means that every career should be a vocation.

All this is implied in the idea of American democracy. It does not describe American educational practice but defines the goal of educational effort. There are many forces which work against it and postpone its realization to the indefinite future: inertia, costs, inequalities of economic condition and of human talent, the general failure of society to do, or to do well, what it ought to do. But this education for choice is the norm of educational criticism and the motive of educational reform in America. For American democracy means that society shall be so organized and directed by its members that they shall live as they choose.

149

Choosing is a burdensome privilege, from which men shrink, and for which they need to be prepared. It means something to speak of "being relieved from the necessity of choosing." There is a rivalry between the cult of security and the cult of freedom — being looked out for, and looking out for oneself.[8] Which goes to prove, if further proof were needed, that American democracy requires effort, and is not a comfortable refuge or a line of least resistance.

9

American equality springs from many sources. In theory it springs from the axioms of the Declaration of Independence, from the doctrine, namely, that *all men alike,* regardless of birth and station, possess within themselves the faculties of control and the claims to social dividends. All men possess the generic attributes of reason and conscience; all men, having interests at stake, are stockholders in the collective enterprise.

In practice and experience, American equalitarianism springs from the spirit of individual self-reliance which activated the colonists and later immigrants, and from the leveling effect of a frontier environment, which superseded prior differences of status in the countries of origin, and which presented all alike with a common task requiring common virtues. These virtues were the elementary virtues of thrift, labor, endurance, courage, sagacity, and sociability, which depend least upon differences of talent or cultural background, and give a positive meaning to the idea of the "common man."

It is no part of the American idea of equality that men should be leveled down, but rather that they should be leveled up. American democracy is a society of rising and not of declining men. Eminence is coveted rather than

8 Cf. Erich Fromm, *Escape from Freedom,* 1941.

disparaged, provided it be earned and deserved, and not created by the social structure itself. The expressions "self-made man" or "from shirt-sleeves to shirt-sleeves" imply a ladder of eminence which may be climbed or descended by the individual according to his capacity. The playing down of differences of caste implies a playing up of individual differences. Freedom and equality of opportunity distribute men on a scale which reflects what they make of opportunity. This is applicable not only to wealth but to political power, as was recognized by the original Jeffersonians:

> A Democracy is beyond all question the freest government: because under this, every man is equally protected by the laws, and has equally a voice in making them. But I do not say an equal voice; because some men have stronger lungs than others, and can express more forcibly their opinions of public affairs. Others, though they may not speak very loud, yet have a faculty of saying more in a short time; and even in the case of others, who speak little or none at all, yet what they do say containing good sense, comes with greater weight; so that all things considered, every citizen, has not, in this sense of the word, an equal voice.[9]

Jacksonian democracy was a Jeffersonian democracy that was taken to mean what it said. At the same time it served to bring to light the dangers inherent in the equalitarian gospel, and seemed to justify the worst fears of the anti-democrats. When men are encouraged to believe that the great and good things of life are within the reach of all, they are inclined to invert the principle, and to believe that what lies within the reach of all is great and good. When achievement requires effort, discipline, and talent, the easy way out is to lower the sights. Those who derive power from popular support will tend to flatter men for

[9] Hugh Henry Brackenridge, *Modern Chivalry* (originally published 1792–1815) , 1937, p. 20.

what they are, rather than disparage them by pointing out their shortcomings.

The demagogues are not limited to politics. They appear in every sphere of life, including manners, business, literature, and the arts, in which popularity is rewarded. Hence the evil of vulgarism, which is not inherent in the idea of democracy but is its besetting sin, in all times and places, America included. New and almost irresistible temptations to this sin are offered by the modern arts of advertising and publicity.

Vulgarism is no part of the idea of American democracy. A perfected American democracy would recognize an equality of courtesy, an equality of generic man before nature or God, an equality of treatment by government and law; and at the same time acknowledge inequalities of talent and personal quality, and welcome the differences of achievement and influence in which these inequalities are reflected. It would define standards and hold them, while at the same time making it possible for as many as possible, and as far as possible, to qualify. In this American democracy fails as well as succeeds.

10

There are two sides of equalitarianism, the near side which is plainly visible, and the far side which requires thought and imagination: "I am equal to you," and "You are equal to me"; "I am equal," and "We are equal." The former judgment may be innocent or even praiseworthy, but it possesses no moral merit. Democracy, and all its shibboleths and catchwords, "the people," "freedom," "liberty," "equality," derive their moral value, and derive it wholly, from the universality and interchangeability of their terms; or, quite simply, from the "Golden Rule," whose triteness does not make it less golden.

In other words American democracy is a moral democracy, and the American people are a moral people. This
has nothing to do with their obedience of moral precepts
— their chastity, temperance, honesty, veracity, dutiful-
ness, or unselfishness — but only with the fact that their
institutions and collective judgments are founded on
moral principle. They do not always live up to it; but if
they do not, they suffer from an uneasy conscience, and
feel the need of reform or of self-justification.

The fundamental moral idea is conveyed by such small
or simple expressions as "all," "every man," and the plural
first-personal pronouns. The control of our affairs is to be
exercised, and their benefits are to be enjoyed, by all, by
every man, by us, severally and inclusively. When Americans are left out, become "forgotten men," or are neglected
or left behind in the march of progress, they have a "just
grievance" and something must be done about it. If they
themselves protest they do so not as supplicants, but as
claimants, demanding that which in some sense is already
theirs.

"Right" is a moral term. It does not signify mere desire.
There are many desires which are not rights. It is quite
true that men are likely to claim as a right what they desire, especially if they are accustomed to having it. In the
American election of 1944 there were many who felt and
spoke as though they had a right to beefsteak. But this
claim was only a way of putting a fair face on greed; or a
way of insisting that there was enough beefsteak to go
around, and that everybody should therefore have his
share. Many men desire to avoid work; nevertheless we
speak of a right to work, and not of a right not to work;
or only of a right to a certain modicum of rest and recrea-
tion. We speak of a right to subsistence, and not of a right
to luxury. The notion of rights, in other words, springs
from the idea that society is a coöperative enterprise, in

which all participate, and from which all shall receive certain minimum benefits.

It is sometimes held that rights are essentially legal, that they have no being unless they are provided for and guaranteed by the civil authority. The American system is a government by law. The legal enforcement of contract is an indispensable condition of collective action. Americans are disposed to take full advantage of their legal rights, as well as to accept their contractual risks and obligations. There are many Americans who have no other personal conscience but the sanction of the law.

But if there were no other rights but legal rights, it would be meaningless to speak of *enacting* rights; that is, of giving a legal sanction to rights which are already valid. It would be impossible to argue that legislation or judicial decisions ought to make provision for rights, or recognize them when it does not. There would be no principles to guide the law-maker, no appeal from the law or in behalf of the law — no ulterior premise beyond the law from which the law could be argued. Rights should then have been embodied in the Constitution, and not in the Declaration of Independence.

A right, then, is a share of the total good of society to which its individual members are *entitled*. It may take the "permissive" form of a good which the individual is allowed to obtain for himself, or the enabling form of a good which society helps him to obtain. In America until recently the emphasis has been on the former rather than the latter class of rights. In any case it is limited, limited in its enjoyment by one individual in order that it may be enjoyed by all individuals. It is bounded, as a share, a portion, an allotment, is bounded. It is a sphere within a system of spheres.

This order of rights is what is familiarly known as "justice" — distributive or social justice, as distinguished from

retributive or punitive justice. The ideas of democracy
partake of moral value when and only when they embody
this principle. This is the moral-social doctrine which,
rather than any metaphysics, or even any religion, can be
said to be the ground on which Americans stand. It is that
"higher law," or "natural law," which Americans recognize as the sanction of their institutions, and as the guiding
principle of public policy. It is the standard by which
Americans condemn Fascism, Nazism, Communism, and
Totalitarianism not as weak or inexpedient, but as wrong.
It links their political judgments with their conscience and
not merely with their prudence.

It is this principle of just rights which links the political
judgments of Americans with their humanitarianism, and
gives a political meaning to concrete charitableness, represented by Jane Addams and Hull House; and by the
social worker, typified by Frances Perkins, when she said
of the Labor Department over which she presided:

> The winter's coal, the plumbing, the interest on the
> mortgage, a good diet, the baby's milk, marriage, and cul-
> tural needs, even soda waters and rides on the pony in the
> park must always precede generalized abstract theory in our
> own thinking. We are chiefly concerned with men and
> women in the process of living and working.[10]

This attitude is not unrelated to the "generalized
theory" in American thinking. It is the intimate and
homely application of that theory, with special concern
for those parts of society which have at any given time
failed to enjoy its benefits. This is the fundamental force
in American reform, in the remorse which is felt for racial
or class discrimination, and in the steadily mounting concern for the health, housing and living conditions, and
economic opportunity, of those who are getting the worst
of the bargain. Americans are morally "shocked," not be-

[10] *Op. cit.*, p. 283.

cause they have failed merely, but because they feel that they have been unfaithful to their own idea of what ought to be.

11

When at the close of the last century America acquired over-seas possessions, and found itself in the unaccustomed rôle of suppressing a war of liberation in the Philippines, the American conscience found expression in an "Anti-Imperialist League," whose platform contained the following statement:

> We regret that it has become necessary in the land of Washington and Lincoln to reaffirm that all men, of whatever race or color, are entitled to life, liberty, and the pursuit of happiness. We maintain that goverments derive their just powers from the consent of the governed. We insist that the subjugation of any people is "criminal aggression" and open disloyalty to the distinctive principles of our Government.[11]

"Anti-imperialism" was a moral protest. While it did not immediately prevail in the Philippines, and has not prevented economic and strategic expansion in various parts of the world, it is impossible for America to be imperialistic with a good conscience. This same scruple has been carried over from isolationism to internationalism. It explains Woodrow Wilson and the ill-fated League of Nations. It explains the moral fervor with which Americans have supported the United Nations and even the idea of World Government.

The moral principles which constitute the American conscience are of universal application. The rights on which the American system is founded are the rights of men as men, regardless of ethnic differences and political fron-

[11] *Speeches, Correspondence and Political Papers of Carl Schurz*, 1913, Vol. VI, p. 77 (note).

tiers. In principle America rejects racism, the corporate state, historical relativism, and the cult of power. It is American, in principle if not in practice, to be concerned with the condition of backward or dependent peoples. There is, in other words, an original allegiance of America, dating from the Age of the Enlightenment, to the ideas of world-wide human welfare through coöperation and local self-determination within a broad framework of tolerance and mutual respect. Americans do not need to be converted to these ideas, but only to learn how to realize them; and here Americans are not inclined to defeatism. Their fault is more likely to lie in their impatience and naïveté, and in their failure to count the costs.

12

Americans are accustomed to count upon the future to make good the failures of the past, and the shortcomings of the present. In their buoyancy of spirits, their sense of movement and growth, their power to make what has to be made and to do what has to be done, the American idea of "destiny" is confirmed by experience. The American people do not feel themselves to be a "chosen people" in any fatalistic sense, as being the embodiment of the Absolute Idea, or the appointed instrument of Providence. Americans are utopian but not apocalyptic. Even the idea of destined greatness has not meant a necessary greatness, decreed in the heavens, but a conditional greatness, arising from a happy conjunction of enlightenment and natural resources — a greatness of opportunity which has to be seized and not passively accepted. It is in this sense that the word "faith" has come to take its place with "democracy," "people," "freedom," and "rights" in the vocabulary of American eloquence. American faith is a faith in man, and nothing is more instinctively and profoundly repugnant to Americans than that contempt for man which has in the present century been proclaimed by Mussolini, Hitler, Lenin, and Stalin.

American faith does not imply complacency. America is known by its evil as well as by its good. The winds of progress blow fitfully, and the ship of democracy is often becalmed or drifts backward. There are dark clouds on the horizon of the future. Action is followed by reaction. Political corruption is notorious. Economic tyrannies spring up in place of the political tyranny which has been feared and avoided. The competitive economy develops hard-heartedness and greed. Poverty, bad housing, disease, and illiteracy still abound. There are ugly manifestations of racial prejudice. Freedom of thought is curtailed in order to root out the enemies of freedom; Dies Committees employ methods ominously similar to those of the "un-Americanism" against which they profess to be directed. Primitive emotions are excited, and clichés are circulated by commercialized agencies of mass-communication; tabloids make the tabloid mind. The possession of industrial and military power tends to generate a display of power in the area of world-politics. From ignorance or ill-will many Americans are unfaithful to the principles of Americanism.

All of these evils, doubts, and dangers are, however, known to Americans, and condemned by Americans. Their removal creates the deepest and most persistent motive of American life. It has created the great eras and the great movements — which have been retarded, but never reversed, in American history. The great American presidents, Washington, Jefferson, Jackson, Lincoln, Wilson, and the two Roosevelts, unlike Charlemagne, Elizabeth, Frederick the Great, Peter the Great, Bismarck, Napoleon, and Hitler, have been admired for their moral qualities and their moral leadership. They have been the voices and the instruments by which the American creed was reaffirmed and carried into practice.

It is essential to America, as perhaps to no other nation in history, that there should be a creed from which to derive a sense of working together in a line defined by tradition and extended to the future; and by which, as the New Testament was founded on the Old, they should combine piety with evangelism. America depends upon such a creed to save her from the excesses of her individualism, and from aimless preoccupation with her technological gadgets. Americans must feel not only that they have a cause, but that they are succeeding. There must be appreciable gains, and not merely a stubborn fidelity.

Democracy suits America eminently well. American democracy does not run smoothly; at best it flounders and lunges ahead. But it suits a people who are neither a mechanism nor an organism, but a collection of mobile and distinct individuals who know how to organize themselves as the given task may require. Democracy does not depend on a rigid discipline, like military or totalitarian discipline, externally imposed, and therefore brittle and precarious. It has its perpetual roots in human nature, and in the permanent temperament and disposition of Americans. It can survive the rise and decline of authorities and the vicissitudes of history.

Since the faith which is here presented is also my own faith, I may be permitted in conclusion to drop into the first personal pronoun, and to say what remains to be said, without argument. The fundamental principles of Americanism seem to me quite simple and trite — individual responsibility, coöperation, intelligence, love, kindness, generosity, sympathy, and the Golden Rule: individual responsibility, that is, dedication of the will to the good as one sees it, and the acceptance of the burden of service;

coöperation, that is, working with others for an end which is greater than any one because it embraces all; intelligence, that is, using one's brains to guide one's hand and one's word; love, that is, caring for others; kindness, that is, manifesting love to others; generosity, that is, giving to others without thought of oneself; sympathy, that is, interchanging feelings with others; the Golden Rule, that is, reckoning each individual in his own terms as having claims similar to one's own.

The principles are simple and trite. But their application is difficult and always new, incapable of perfect achievement, and inducing humility in any one who holds the principles high and measures himself by them. And their application is complicated and tortuous, requiring all the faculties, arts, and technologies at human command. This is what I think to be most profoundly American and most profoundly human — the striving and the contriving, with the hope that one may gain something in the right direction, and with the assurance that if one fails it will not be by default but because of the greatness of the cause.

Acknowledgments

THE AUTHOR wishes to acknowledge his indebtedness to publishers and individuals who have given permission to quote passages from the following books or articles:

The American Book Company: H. H. Brackenridge, *Modern Chivalry;* and *The American Mind,* edited by H. R. Warfel, R. H. Gabriel, and S. T. Williams.

The John Day Company: Frances Perkins, *People at Work.*

E. P. Dutton and Company: Allen S. Will, *Life of Cardinal Gibbons,* 1922; and Van Wyck Brooks, *Sketches in Criticism,* 1932.

Henry Pratt Fairchild, *The Melting-Pot Mistake.*

Harper & Brothers: S. L. Clemens, *Life on the Mississippi;* and Gunnar Myrdal, *An American Dilemma.*

The Harvard University Press: Ralph Barton Perry, *Thought and Character of William James* (Briefer Version).

Houghton Mifflin Company: Henry David Thoreau, *Miscellanies;* and Ralph Waldo Emerson, *Essays* and *Journals.*

Miss Mildred Howells and John Mead Howells: William Dean Howells, *Criticism and Fiction.*

Alfred A. Knopf: Timothy Flint, *Recollections of the Last Ten Years.*

The Macmillan Company: passages quoted in Philip Hughes, *The Pope's New Order,* 1944; and in Ryan and Boland, *Catholic Principles of Politics,* copyright 1940 by The National Catholic Welfare Conference.

Charles E. Merriam, *History of American Political Theories.*

Random House: *The Public Papers and Addresses of Franklin Delano Roosevelt.*

Characteristically American

Paul R. Reynolds & Son: William James, *The Meaning of Truth*.

Charles Scribner's Sons: Rev. F. X. Talbot, S.J., "Catholicism in America," *America Now*, edited by H. E. Stearns.

Index

i

Index

Index

Index

Index

A NOTE ON THE TYPE USED IN THIS BOOK

The text of this book has been set on the Linotype in a type-face called "Baskerville." The face is a facsimile reproduction of types cast from molds made for John Baskerville (1706–1775) from his designs. The punches for the revived Linotype Baskerville were cut under the supervision of the English printer George W. Jones.

John Baskerville's original face was one of the forerunners of the type-style known as "modern face" to printers: a "modern" of the period A.D. 1800.

The book was composed, printed, and bound by The Plimpton Press, Norwood, Massachusetts.